YO-BTB-536

The Market for
Financial Services

NOUS-SOMMES-PRETS

SIMON FRASER UNIVERSITY

W.A.C. BENNETT LIBRARY

THE ECONOMICS
OF THE SERVICE SECTOR
IN CANADA

Series Editors:
Herbert G. Grubel
Michael A. Walker

The Market for Financial Services

Deposit-Taking
Institutions

John F. Chant

This study is part of a general programme of research into the services sector made possible by a contribution from the Department of Regional Industrial Expansion, Government of Canada.

Canadian Cataloguing in Publication Data

Chant, John F., 1937

   The market for financial services: deposit-

taking institutions

   (The Economics of the service sector in

Canada, ISSN 0835-4227)

   Bibliography: p.

   ISBN 0-88975-126-9

   1. Deposit banking - Canada. 2. Banks and

banking - Canada. 3. Trust companies -

Canada. 4. Credit unions - Canada.

I . Fraser Institute (Vancouver, B.C.). II. Title. III Series.

HG1660.C2C53 1988   332.1'752'0971   C88-091373-8

Printed in Singapore.

CONTENTS

Tables and Figures

Tables

Figures

PREFACE AND SUMMARY

Recently, much attention has been directed towards the service industries and their implications for the economy. The deposit-taking sector, a particularly important service industry, has been frequently studied in terms of regulation and its effect on the safety and soundness of financial institutions. This study, in contrast, treats the deposit-taking sector as an industry from the same perspective as any other industry i.e. as a producer of output and an employer of labour. It also addresses many of the current issues of concern about the growth of the service sector.

Chapter 1 introduces the topic of this study. Chapter 2 presents an overview of the structure and organization of the deposit-taking sector. It examines the services supplied by this sector and its major customers. It also compares the components of the industry—the chartered banks, the trust and loan companies and the credit unions—in terms of their form of organization, their size, and the role of associated enterprises and foreign ownership. Finally, it notes the significance of regulation in shaping the industry.

Chapter 3 examines recent trends in the output and productivity in the deposit-taking sector. Criticisms of the conceptual basis of current "imputed" measures of the output of this sector are examined. The analysis concludes that present methods are consistent with a "flow-through" approach to the measurement of capital income. The quantitative analysis shows that over the years 1973 to 1983 the growth of GNP in the deposit-taking sector at market prices exceeded that of the rest of the economy by 1 percent per year. At the same time, the rate of price increase in the deposit-taking sector fell below that of the rest of the economy by .8 percent. As a consequence, growth of real GNP in the deposit-taking sector exceeded that of the rest of the economy by approximately 1.6 percent.

Chapter 4 reviews employment and earnings in the deposit-taking sector. As is the case of much information about the sector, it is difficult to find consistent data for employment and earnings. Employment in the deposit-taking sector showed substantial growth from 1960 to 1980 followed by a lack of growth in the 1980s. Overall, both banks and other financial institutions substantially increased their share of industrial employment. At the same time, the average earnings in the sector increased by 23 percent relative to the earnings in the service sector overall and by 25 percent relative to industrial earnings. The change in average earnings was accompanied by an improvement in the skills of employees and the organization and salary levels of the employment offered in the sector.

The tax treatment of the deposit-taking sector is examined in Chapter 5. While the deposit-taking sector is subject to the corporate income tax in the same way as other sectors, the activities of the sector affect the impact of the taxes. Most notably, deposit-taking institutions have reduced their taxes through participating in "after-tax" financing. On the other hand, chartered banks are subject to capital taxes and reserve requirements, the equivalent to a tax, that are not applied to other sectors.

Chapter 6 studies the profits and costs of the deposit-taking sector. Profit measures for the sector present a paradox. Accounting measures show lower rates of profit for the deposit-taking sector than for the rest of the economy. On the other hand, the returns realized by shareholders have been consistently superior to that of the Toronto 300 Index. Accounting and stock return measures agree that the returns in the deposit-taking sector are less variable than the rest of the economy. Differences between the activities of the deposit-taking sector and the rest of the economy limit the usefulness of cost comparisons. As might be expected, deposit-taking institutions spend more on interest expense and less on materials than other sectors. When only expenses related to value-added are considered, non financial business spends a greater proportion than the deposit-taking sector on all categories except bond interest and other expenses.

The extensive and rapid innovations in the deposit-taking sector and their causes are reviewed in Chapter 7. The analysis also shows the ways in which innovations such as bank cards, automated banking machines, daily interest accounts and point-of-sale terminals have affected deposit-taking institutions and their customers.

In Chapter 8, public policy within the deposit-taking sector is discussed. Service sector policy can be distinguished from policy in the prudential regulation of financial institutions. The study reviews a number of general concerns that have been expressed about the effects of the growth of the service sector and finds that the performance of the deposit-taking sector does not appear to justify policy measures to meet these concerns. Quality of employment appears to have improved, technical change has reduced the close locational ties between the production and use of financial services, and innovation tends to benefit consumers and does not appear to threaten the state of competition. On the other hand, concern is expressed about the current state of prudential regulation. The study concludes with a number of suggestions that would have the potential to enhance competition in financial markets without endangering the safety and stability of the system.

ACKNOWLEDGEMENTS

I wish to thank Robert Frindt for his skilled research assistance and Jack Galbraith, Randy Geehan, Herb Grubel and Tom Rymes for their useful comments.

ABOUT THE AUTHOR

John Chant teaches at Simon Fraser University where he specializes in monetary economics. He received his B.A. from the University of British Columbia and his Ph.D. from Duke University. He taught at the University of Edinburgh, Queen's University and Carleton University before coming to Simon Fraser. In addition, he served as Research Director of the Financial Markets Group at the Economic Council of Canada that produced the study, *Efficiency and Regulation*, which was an important input to the Bank Act of 1980. He is the author of several books including *The Allocative Effects of Inflation* and *The Economics of the Canadian Financial System: Theory, Policy and Institutions* and numerous articles on monetary policy and the regulation of financial institutions. Professor Chant, as one of the foremost experts in Canada on the regulation of financial institutions, has served as a consultant to the Bank of Canada, the Commission of Inquiry into Residential Tenancies, and the Royal Commission on the Economic Union and Development Prospects for Canada. Most recently he has been advising the Government of Indonesia, through the Harvard Institute of International Development, with respect to the regulation of its banking system.

Chapter 1

INTRODUCTION

This study examines a set of financial institutions, referred to collectively as deposit-taking institutions, that consists of chartered banks, trust companies, mortgage loan companies and credit unions. These deposit-taking institutions supply the majority of the money used by households and businesses to carry out their transactions. They also channel the funds of savers into the hands of borrowers who can use them productively. Finally, deposit-taking institutions transmit the effects of monetary policy to other sectors of the economy. These institutions have been prominent as a concern of public policy because of their pervasive role in the economy.

Deposit-taking institutions have been studied endlessly from the perspective of public policy in recent years. Failures of trust companies and then chartered banks have called into question the present system of regulation and deposit insurance. This study examines deposit-taking institutions from a different perspective. It views the deposit-taking sector as a service industry and asks the same questions as are being asked about other service industries and the service sector in general. Has the deposit-taking sector grown relative to the rest of the economy? If so, what has caused its growth? What are the implications of a growing service sector for the Canadian economy? For the quality of employment? For the prospects of innovation?

The threads of these different approaches to the deposit-taking sector cannot be completely disentangled. The essential characteristics of the sector cannot be ignored even when considering it as a service sector. While many of the concerns raised about the deposit-taking sector will be the same as for the restaurant industry, for example, many will not. It is not the purpose of this study to once again review the regulation of deposit-taking institutions, but in many instances the issues cannot be avoided. As the study progressed, a number of common themes emerged in the examination of the diverse aspects of the activity of deposit taking.

The shape and structure of the industry are the creation of regulation to a greater degree than almost any other industry. Regulation defines the activities of deposit-taking institutions and determines who can participate in them. Changes in regulation, as demonstrated by the revamping of security trading that occurred effective June 30, 1987, can dramatically alter seemingly permanent features of the industry.

The industry has also undergone a thorough revolution in its character over the past two decades with the impetus being innovation made possible through changing communication and computer technology. This revolution has shaped the product, changed the employment conditions, and altered the organization of the industry and the firms within it.

Finally, the deposit-taking sector does not appear to fit many of the stereotypes of a service industry. As already mentioned, it has undergone extensive innovation and technical change. In addition, while it has grown in importance in the economy as an employer, this growth has been accompanied by a raising of the skills and incomes of its employees relative to other workers.

Chapter 2

THE DEPOSIT-TAKING
SECTOR: AN OVERVIEW

The deposit-taking sector consists of the group of financial institutions that includes chartered banks, trust companies, deposit-accepting mortgage loan companies, and credit unions and *caisses populaires*. This set of institutions makes up a logical group for study and examination because they share the common characteristic that they accept funds in the form of deposits from the general public and, as a consequence, can be distinguished from other elements of the financial industry.

These institutions are financial intermediaries in that they collect funds from one part of the public and lend them to another. They can, as a result, be distinguished from market intermediaries that operate to bring demanders and suppliers of financial instruments together without issuing claims themselves to the demanders of financial instruments. These market intermediaries include investment dealers and brokers.

The financial institutions that are the subject of this study differ from other financial institutions such as pension funds and insurance companies by the nature of their liabilities. Deposit institutions collect the majority of their funds through the issue of deposits, claims of fixed money value that are repayable on agreed terms, though generally of short duration. Other financial institutions offer different types of claims. Insurance companies offer claims that require them to make payments upon certain contingencies, such as death or an accident. Pension funds issue claims to income upon retirement, and mutual funds offer claims that have their value tied to the value of the portfolio held by the fund.

Deposit-taking institutions are classified in the Standard Industrial Classification of 1980 as major group 70, Deposit-Accepting Intermediary Industries, within Division K, Finance and Insurance Industries. Within this major group are six subgroups: 701, central bank; 702, chartered banks and other banking type intermediaries; 703, trust companies; 704, deposit-accepting mortgage companies; 705, credit unions; and 709, other deposit-accepting intermediaries.

The statistics compiled on the deposit-taking industry are probably as comprehensive as any other industrial sector. Deposit-taking institutions are typically represented in all general industrial statistics such as employment and earnings, corporate balance sheets and other financial data, and investment and capital. Because of its role in financing other economic activity and in the transmission of monetary policy, the deposit-taking industry also has its activity reported intensively in specialized statistical releases. This sector is treated separately as a subsector in the financial flow accounts, whereas non-financial industries are classed together as business enterprises. Measures are presented on the level of payments activity and rate of turnover of deposit accounts issued by banks. The Bank of Canada collects and publishes both weekly and monthly balance sheet data for the chartered banks. Chartered banks are required to file monthly returns on their financial condition and annual reports on their income and expenses that are published on an individual bank basis in the *Canada Gazette,* and the balance sheets and income and expense statements of individual trust and mortgage loan companies are published by some provincial authorities.[1] While some of this information is also published for some other financial institutions, the frequency of reporting appears to be unique for the chartered banks, and this detailed publication of data for individual enterprises appears to be unparalleled outside the financial sector.

A major problem in the study of the deposit-taking sector arises, despite the comprehensiveness of the data available for the industry, because of conceptual problems in the measurement of the industry's output. As will be discussed more fully in chapter 3, national income accountants are forced to resort to imputing much of the output of the sector from the spreads between the interest rates received and paid by deposit-taking institutions. These spreads measure in total the amounts that customers are willing to pay for the services, but they do not indicate the amounts that borrowers and lenders are willing to pay separately for the services. In addition, the imputation does not indicate the different services and their respective prices and quantities that make up the imputed output for the sector.

This problem with data limits a number of the questions that can be explored in this study. Study of the sources of demand for the product becomes limited by the inability to determine the specific services, and their prices, that have been purchased by borrowers and lenders in using the services of deposit-taking institutions. By the same token, any attempt to study the input/output relationships for this industry encounters the same problems.

SERVICES OF DEPOSIT-TAKING INSTITUTIONS

Deposit-taking institutions provide services to two types of customers: their depositors and their borrowers. Depositors gain services because of the characteristics of deposits relative to the other forms in which they could hold their wealth. Borrowers receive services to the extent that they can gain credit more cheaply through borrowing from a bank than from alternative sources. In addition, deposit-taking institutions offer a variety of other services that are closely related to their major services. The range of services offered by deposit-taking institutions is presented in table 1.

Services to Depositors

Depositors receive payments services, liquidity services and portfolio management services from holding deposits. Many bank deposits, in particular demand deposits and other chequable deposits, serve as an important element of the means of payment in the economy. Holders of these deposits are able to transfer them to others as payment for the goods and services that they purchase. While currency and coin can also be used to make payments, the transfer of bank deposits has clear advantages for the payment of large sums and for payments across distances.

Closely related to the payments services are the liquidity services rendered by banks. Holders of bank deposits acquire an asset with different characteristics than the underlying assets held by the deposit institutions. Bank deposits are fixed in money value and can be of different maturity and denomination than the assets held by the banks. Thus, depositors are able to hold an asset with characteristics that more closely meet their needs than would the underlying assets. Bank depositors also gain general portfolio management services from deposit institutions. The deposit holder is relieved from the need to make portfolio decisions. The financial institution screens and supervises investments on behalf of its depositors. The depositor receives a fixed return, agreed upon in advance, independent of the performance of the underlying portfolio held by the financial institution.

Services to Borrowers

Borrowers gain services from deposit institutions to the extent that they are able to borrow more easily from the institution than they could on their own. When borrowers attempt to borrow from ultimate lenders, they must supply information about themselves and their enterprises so that potential lenders can assess the risks and returns involved. Borrowers differ in terms of the cost involved to them in assembling the data required by lenders. Large

Table 1
Services Offered by Deposit-Taking Institutions

	Chartered Banks	Trust Companies	Credit Unions
Lending			
Mortgage loans	X	X	X
Other loans to individuals	X	X	X
Business loans and financing	X	X	X
Loans to provinces and municipal or school corporations	X	X	
Deposit-Taking and Currency Exchange	X	X	X
Households' deposits	X	X	X
Commercial deposits	X	X	X
Cash management accounts	X	—	
Currency exchange	X	X	X
Safekeeping facilities	X	X	X
Automatic teller machines	X	X	X
Travellers' cheques	X	X	X
Market Intermediation			
Full brokerage	?	?	?
Discount brokerage	X	?	?
Underwriting of new issues	—	—	—
Specialized Business Financing			
Venture capital financing	X	—	X
Merchant banking	X	—	X
Financial leasing	X	X	X
Lease factoring	X	X	X
Factoring	X		X
Export and import financing	X	X	X
Information and Advisory Services			
Information on the economic situation	X	X	X
Cash management consulting for enterprises	X	—	X
Investment counselling	—	X	—
Financial planning	—	X	X
Other Services			
Fund mutualization	X	X	—
Securitization	—	X	—

Source: *A Framework for Financial Regulation*, Economic Council, p. 40.

enterprises that frequently use capital markets to raise funds may be able to develop staff that specialize in information gathering and dissemination. Smaller firms and individuals are less likely to be skilled at this task. Deposit institutions, in their lending role, relieve borrowers from this burden by specializing in the assessment of borrowers and their prospects. By using the intermediary, many borrowers are able to borrow at cheaper cost, especially when transacting costs are added to interest costs, from financial institutions than they could by borrowing directly from ultimate lenders.

Other Services

The banking services described so far are fundamental to the process of intermediation and are performed as the major activity of deposit-taking institutions. In addition, each of the institutions performs a variety of other functions.

In one case, that of trust companies, the other functions they perform come close to rivalling intermediation in importance as their primary activity. This other activity carried on by trust companies consists of their trust business, more formally known as the estate, trust and agency business, in which the trust companies manage assets on behalf of others. The essential difference between the trustee business and the intermediary business is that the trust assets are only administered by the trust company and remain under the ownership of their customers, whereas in their intermediary business the assets are owned by the intermediary which, in turn, has a liability to its depositors.

The other services offered by financial institutions cover a wide range. Some are related to the key role of the intermediaries in the foreign exchange market: they buy and sell foreign currencies, issue travellers' cheques and arrange other types of international payments. Financial institutions also offer safekeeping through safety deposit boxes and other facilities for the safekeeping of securities. They assist their customers to sell and purchase securities, including acting as agents for the sale of Canada Savings Bonds. Most deposit-taking institutions issue credit cards to their customers, and many sell their customers other financial services such as insurance and tax-sheltered investment plans. Finally, many deposit-taking institutions have begun to offer new techniques for borrowing to their larger corporate customers. Through interest rate swaps, financial institutions arrange terms and conditions of payments that suit the needs of borrowers better than would be possible under simple transactions. Through securitization, financial institutions package the borrowings of their customers to make them more attractive to direct lenders. In effect, the financial institution becomes an arranger of loans rather than an intermediary between the ultimate lenders and borrowers.

USERS OF FINANCIAL SERVICES

The main users of the financial services supplied by deposit institutions are households and business enterprises. On the deposit side, the emphasis on different services differs between the two groups. Households are the most important source of funds for deposit-taking institutions. At the end of 1985, approximately 80 percent of total deposits at deposit-taking institutions were held by households or unincorporated businesses. Households hold deposits as a major form of accumulation of savings. Approximately 75 percent of these funds are held in accounts that do not have chequing privileges. In addition, households gain payment services by writing cheques against their accounts. Businesses emphasize more the payments services that are required for paying their employees and purchasing other inputs. While the proportion of business accounts that have chequing privileges is quite close to that of households, the turnover of these accounts is many times greater. Businesses also use the wholesale deposits of deposit institutions as a form for investing temporary accumulations of cash. In this role, the deposit institutions have to compete with a variety of other issuers of short-term financial instruments.

A different pattern emerges on the lending side of the business of deposit-taking institutions. At the end of 1985, businesses borrowed $89.4 billion from the deposit-taking sector through loans, whereas households borrowed only $48.8 billion. Households, on the other hand, accounted for approximately $90 million of $110 million mortgages held by deposit-taking institutions.

Household Demand for Deposit-Taking Services

From the point of view of the household, financial services have two significant features which must be taken into account. First, unlike many goods and services purchased by households, financial services cannot be considered as directly being part of the household's consumption but rather must be considered as intermediate inputs that improve the consumption possibilities available to the household. Secondly, household labour must be combined with financial services in many instances to produce the desired increase in consumption. Each of these points is elaborated more fully.

Benefits from Deposit-Taking Services

Some services purchased by households can be clearly regarded as consumption goods. Attendance at movies, the use of a golf course, and styling at hairdressers give direct satisfaction to the purchaser in that the entertainment, the recreation and the improved appearance are ends in themselves. Financial services, however, are not ends in themselves. These services improve the welfare of households indirectly by making a wider range of opportunities available to them.

The financial services industry supplies two types of services to households: payments services and store of value services. Payments services permit households to more efficiently exchange the goods and services they produce for the goods and services they wish to consume. Without these payments services, households would be limited to using currency for making transactions. While currency may be the most efficient way of making many transactions and may not be appreciably inferior for other transactions, it is extremely inefficient for some. The acquisition of a house, the sale of labour services on a regular basis, and purchase of stocks or bonds all represent transactions which would be extremely costly if carried out through currency. Excess costs would arise from the need to provide security, the transportation of the currency from buyer to seller, and the need to count the currency tendered in the transaction.

The services provided to households through the store of value function are even less tangible. Households are unlikely to wish to consume exactly the amount of their current income. Among the factors that may cause consumption to depart from current income are age and family status. Households tend to save little in the early and final stages of their lifetimes. In the early stages, their income is relatively low and their need to build up a stock of consumer durables requires households to save little or go into debt. Households may save little or even dissave in old age because they no longer receive any income from labour services. In contrast, households in the middle stages of life tend to consume less than their current income and either pay off their accumulated debts or acquire assets to provide for their old age.

Households would be severely limited in their choices in the absence of financial markets and financial assets. They would be confined in their choice of stores of value to acquiring real assets that are subject to deterioration, costs of storage, and the need for security. Moreover, the household would need to find a willing buyer for the asset at the time it wishes to consume again. Financial assets permit the households to transfer resources to other households or enterprises in return for claims to future resources. The more sophisticated the financial markets, the greater is the range of choices available to households.

Use of Household Labour

The second important characteristic of financial services—one shared by many other services—is that it requires the use of the consumer's labour in order to produce the desired service. The household desiring to make payments must arrange for the deposit of adequate funds into the bank and, subsequently, must transfer cheques to payees where this mode of payment is being used or withdraw the cash if payment is going to be made in currency. Less labour must be expended by households in gaining the store of value services of financial institutions. These services are obtained by merely holding the claims issued by the financial institutions.

The need for customers to combine labour with financial services in order to gain the desired services is especially important for the purposes of this study in that it places a perspective on the effects of innovations in the financial sector. The effects of an innovation on the use of labour must be considered with respect to the total labour used to produce financial services. An innovation can be labour saving even if it does not reduce the labour used by financial institutions to produce their services if it reduces the labour required from customers. By the same token, changes that reduce the labour requirements of financial institutions can be labour using if they increase the labour used by customers by a greater amount.

STRUCTURE OF THE INDUSTRY

Components of the Sector

Four separate components of the deposit-taking sector need to be distinguished in examining industrial structure: Schedule A, domestically-owned chartered banks; Schedule B, foreign-owned chartered banks; trust and mortgage loan companies; and credit unions. The characteristics of these enterprises, the rules governing their activities and elements of their business, differ sufficiently that each should be considered separately.

Schedule A chartered banks are granted broad banking powers under the federal Bank Act. A bank must be no more than 25 percent foreign owned and have no more than 10 percent ownership by one interest in order to qualify as a Schedule A bank. At the end of 1986, eight Schedule A banks operated over 7,000 branch offices throughout Canada. As can be seen from table 2, the six largest Schedule A banks are large banks by any standard and all operate extensive networks of branches.[2]

Schedule B chartered banks are those that fail to meet the ownership requirements for Schedule A banks. All of the more than 50 Schedule B chartered banks are the wholly-owned subsidiaries of foreign banks.[3] Schedule B banks are subject to restrictions that do not apply to Schedule A banks with respect to branch offices, size of each bank and total size as a group.

Table 2

Major Chartered Banks

	Total Assets (billions of $)	Branches
Royal	99.6	1,438
Montreal	87.2	1,192
Commerce	80.8	1,538
Nova Scotia	64.0	1,016
Toronto-Dominion	55.5	979
National	27.9	558

Sources: Canadian Bankers' Association, Financial Statistics, 1986, and Canadian Payments
Association, Directory, vol. 1, 1986.

Note: Assets as of October 31, 1986, and branches as of December 31, 1985.

Trust and mortgage loan companies include a variety of different types of institutions. Some are large institutions rivalling the Schedule A banks in size and offering a comprehensive range of services. Some are small local institutions that concentrate on only several aspects of the business, and some are wholly-owned subsidiaries of other financial institutions that serve as a medium for carrying specialized business for the parent. At the end of 1986, 100 trust companies and mortgage loan companies were listed as having deposit insurance coverage under the Canada Deposit Insurance Corporation.

Trust companies engage in two different types of business: an intermediary business where they collect deposits from the public and a trustee business where they administer assets owned by others. Some trust companies specialize in the intermediary business, some specialize in the trustee business, and some do both. Only the intermediary business of trust companies is considered in this study.

Mortgage loan companies are very similar to trust companies except that they cannot engage in trustee activities. Some mortgage loan companies are wholly owned by and are essentially the mortgage lending arms of chartered banks. For the purpose of this study, these bank subsidiaries are considered as part of the banking sector. Like the trust companies, the remaining mortgage loan companies embrace a wide range of sizes.

Credit unions are distinctly different in their organization from other deposit-taking institutions. They are co-operatives owned by members who are also their customers. Unlike other deposit-taking institutions, each credit union is confined to operating in its own province. A few credit unions have deposits of over $100 million and a number of branch offices and offer services to the consumer that are comparable to those at a bank. The majority of credit unions are much smaller with only one office, with some operating only a few hours a week and having no more than $100,000 in deposits. Local credit unions are able to offset the disadvantages of their small size by relying on the services of their provincial central for the investment of funds, access to liquidity when needed and for bookkeeping and other services. In turn, the provincial centrals are able to gain services from the national organization, the Canadian Co-operative Credit Society.

Forms of Organization

Deposit-accepting institutions can be organized as limited liability corporations, co-operatives and government agencies. All chartered banks and trust and loan companies are corporations, whereas all credit unions are organized as co-operatives. The two government agencies are the Treasury Branches of the province of Alberta and the Savings Offices of the province of Ontario.

The relative importance of the different forms of organization differs substantially among the components of the sector. Numerically, the co-operative is the predominant form of organization; 3,500 separate co-operatives operate as credit unions whereas only 170 separate enterprises are organized as corporations. The number of each type of organization fails to measure their importance in terms of volume of business. In 1985, the co-operatives operating as credit unions accounted for only $43.6 billion (8 percent) of the $562 billion of assets held by deposit-accepting institutions. Even smaller were the two government agencies that accounted for just $10.2 billion, or less than 2 percent of industry assets. Corporations account for the remaining 90 percent of the industry.

Size Distribution of Firms

Tables 3 and 4 give a clear indication of the importance of different sized firms.[4] Larger enterprises account for an extremely substantial proportion of the assets of the industry. Five institutions with assets of over $50 billion account for over two-thirds of the industry's assets; the eight institutions with over $20 billion assets have three-quarters of the assets, and the 27 firms with more than $1 billion have almost seven-eighths of the assets.

Larger institutions appear to have a number of features that might put them at an advantage in the deposit-accepting business. Among the factors that could contribute to a size advantage are the scope for diversification, the use of computer technology, and the effects of government regulations.

Effective intermediation requires that institutions assemble portfolios with a sufficient range of assets so as to provide diversification of risk. Historical-

Table 3

Size Distribution of Deposit-Accepting Institutions, 1985

(in billions of dollars)

Asset Size	Banks	Trust and Loan Companies	Credit Unions	Other
Greater than $50 billion	5	0	0	0
	Royal $99.6 Montreal $87.1 Commerce $80.8 N.S. $64.0 T.D. $51.5			
Greater than $10 billion	1	2	0	0
	National $27.8	Canada $21.6 Royal $13.5		
Greater than $5 billion	1	1	0	1
	Continental $5.5	National $8.7		Montreal City & District $6.0
Greater than $1 billion	8	6	1	1
			Vancity	Province of Alberta Treasury Branches
Greater than $500 million	16	5	0	1
				Province of Ontario Savings Office
Greater than $300 million	15	2	7	0

Source: *The Financial Post 500,* summer, 1986.

Table 4

Proportion of Assets Held by Size Group, 1985

(in billions of dollars)

Asset Size	Chartered Banks		Trust and Loan		Credit Unions		Other		Totals	
	Assets	Share of bank assets	Assets (1)	Share of trust and loan assets	Assets	Share of credit union assets	Assets	Share of other assets	Total assets	Share of total assets
Greater than $50 billion	$382.9	87.9%		0.0%		0.0%		0.0%	$382.9	68.0%
Greater than $10 billion	$ 27.7	6.4%	$34.1	46.7%		0.0%		0.0%	$ 61.8	11.0%
Greater than $5 billion	$ 5.5	1.3%	$ 8.7	11.9%		0.0%	$6.0	55.0%	$ 20.2	3.6%
Greater than $1 billion	$ 15.1	3.5%	$15.8	21.6%	$1.3	3.0%	$4.2	38.5%	$ 36.4	6.5%
Greater than $500 million	$ 11.4	2.6%	$11.4	15.6%		0.0%		0.0%	$ 22.8	4.1%
Greater than $300 million	$ 6.3	1.4%	$ 0.8	1.1%	$2.9	6.7%	$0.7	6.4%	$ 10.7	1.9%

Source: *The Financial Post 500* Returns of the Chartered Banks to the Minister of Finance Statistics Canada, Financial Institutions, various dates.

Note: (1) Assets of trust companies do not include estate, trust and agency business.

ly, each of the largest firms in the industry grew out of a series of consolidations of regionally based institutions. The experience was repeated during the mid-1980s, when a number of smaller banks merged with other banks because of loss of confidence from their customers. The mergers and other absorptions during the 1980s alone include Bank of B.C. by Hong Kong and Shanghai Bank in 1986, the Continental Bank by Citibank in 1986, and the Mercantile Bank by the National Bank in 1985. In addition, two smaller banks, the Canadian Commercial Bank and the Northland Bank, were liquidated in 1985.

More recently, a further factor has emerged to increase the advantages of larger institutions. Experience in both Canada and the United States suggests that regulators, while willing to permit the failure of small financial institutions, find the failure of large institutions to be unacceptable. Customers who hold deposits in excess of the limits to deposit insurance appear to come to expect that these deposits are insured *de facto* if held with a large institution. This implicit deposit insurance assists larger institutions to gain corporate deposits both domestically and in international markets.

A further factor of increasing importance in determining the effectiveness of different size enterprises has been greater international influence in financial markets. Size is probably more important in international than in domestic competition. Large firms are more likely to seek the additional business made possible through international activity. In addition, as firms move away from their home market where they have an established reputation, they will find themselves judged to a greater degree on their overall size.

Many observers anticipated that the introduction of the computer into the financial industry would give a greater advantage to larger institutions. In some cases (daily interest accounts, interchange among ATMs and semi-monthly mortgage payments), smaller institutions have proved to be the innovators in the use of computers to provide new services to customers.

Computer technology has failed to have the predicted effect for two main reasons. First, the technology has proved to be more divisible than had initially been expected. In the mid-1970s, future technology in banking appeared to require large mainframe computers. As computer technology evolved through the 1980s, the mini- and micro-computers gave smaller institutions more flexibility to meet their needs. Secondly, and equally important, smaller institutions, in particular the credit unions, exhibited an ability to co-operate in obtaining new technology. Provincial centrals offered centralized bookkeeping to locals by the early 1970s and developed an interchangeable cash card for use in ATMs.

The Role of Associated Enterprises

The various sectors of the deposit-taking industry differ substantially in the importance of the association of the firms in that sector with other enterprises. In addition, the differences have been changing rapidly.

Chartered banks

Prior to 1967, many of the chartered banks owned major portions of the largest trust and loan companies and shared common directors. The revisions to the Bank Act in 1967 required banks to limit their ownership to less than 10 percent of the shares of trust and loan companies and prohibited any overlap between the boards of directors for banks and other financial institutions. At the same time, a 10 percent limit was placed on the ownership of any chartered bank by a common interest. These measures in combination have precluded any ownership links between major chartered banks and other financial institutions.[5]

The chartered banks have also been limited in their ability to own nonfinancial enterprises as part of a conscious policy to maintain a separation between the real and financial sectors. The Bank Act states explicitly that "a bank shall not own shares in a Canadian corporation in any number that would, under the voting rights attached to the shares owned by the bank, permit the bank to vote more than ten per cent of the total votes that could, under the voting rights attached to all the shares of the corporation issued and outstanding, be voted by the holders thereof" [Section 193(2)].

In 1984, chartered banks started a looser form of association in order to offer services to their customers that the banks could not offer directly. In the celebrated Green Line case, the Toronto-Dominion Bank won the right to offer stock trading services to their customers through the auspices of a discount brokerage firm. These powers were extended in early 1987 when Quebec, Ontario and B.C. all permitted investment firms to be owned by chartered banks and other financial institutions. The federal government and the government of Ontario have agreed that chartered banks will be permitted to participate in the securities industry in that province starting June 30, 1987.[6]

Trust and loan companies

Many of the trust and loan companies had a substantial portion of their shares held by chartered banks up to the time of the 1967 Bank Act. As already mentioned, changes to the Bank Act at that time required each bank to reduce its holding of any trust or loan company below 10 percent of the outstanding shares.

Unlike the chartered banks, the trust and loan companies have never been subject to any limitations on the proportion of their shares that could be held by one interest. Indeed, in the period in which the banks were required to reduce their holdings of trust companies, foreign financial interests acquired substantial shareholdings in several trust companies to serve as a substitute for a presence in banking that was denied by the Bank Act. As might be expected, these holdings were disposed of once direct entry into banking was permitted by the 1980 Bank Act.

At the beginning of the 1980s, most of the largest trust companies were independent of other financial institutions or industrial groups. This situation has been reversed by developments from 1980 onward. Table 5 shows the affiliation of major trust companies with their respective financial groupings. Each of the three largest trust companies identified in table 3 was at least 20 percent owned by one of the groupings: Royal Trust by Trilon, Canada Trust by Imasco, and National by E-L Financial. In addition, each of the two next largest trust companies was also part of a financial group (Montreal Trust, Power Corporation; and Guaranty Trust, Central Capital Group). In total, these five largest trust companies that are associated with financial or industrial groupings account for almost 70 percent of industry assets.

Credit unions

The organization of the credit union industry has explicitly incorporated affiliations among firms in the industry. The co-operative theme of the credit union at the local level that brings individual members together is repeated by the relationship between local credit unions and their centrals. Almost every local credit union belongs to a provincial central, and most of the provincial centrals belong in turn to the national association of centrals. These relationships have been fostered to offset the limitations imposed by the size of the typical local credit union. The centrals can provide the locals with computerized bookkeeping services, a wide range of investment outlets, and liquidity assistance when required. In addition, centrals have made it possible for locals to offer their customers access to credit cards, networks of ATMs, trust services and a variety of other financial services. While these affiliations of credit unions have proved useful for the locals and their members, the total assets of local credit unions remain smaller than the size of any one of the five largest banks.

Table 5
Major Financial Groupings

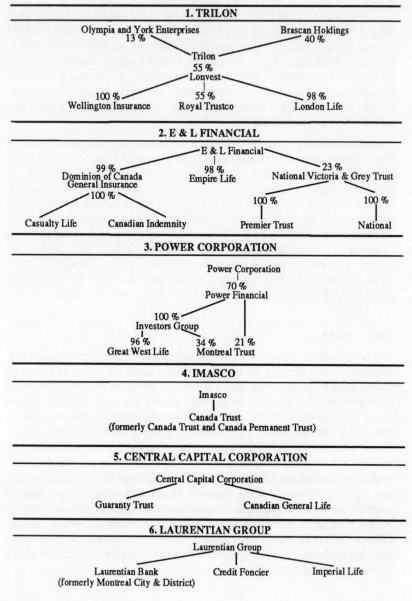

1. TRILON

Olympia and York Enterprises
13 %

Brascan Holdings
40 %

Trilon
55 %
Lonvest

100 %
Wellington Insurance

55 %
Royal Trustco

98 %
London Life

2. E & L FINANCIAL

E & L Financial

99 %
Dominion of Canada
General Insurance
100 %

98 %
Empire Life

23 %
National Victoria & Grey Trust

100 %
Premier Trust

100 %
National

Casualty Life   Canadian Indemnity

3. POWER CORPORATION

Power Corporation
70 %
Power Financial

100 %
Investors Group

96 %
Great West Life

34 %   21 %
Montreal Trust

4. IMASCO

Imasco

Canada Trust
(formerly Canada Trust and Canada Permanent Trust)

5. CENTRAL CAPITAL CORPORATION

Central Capital Corporation

Guaranty Trust   Canadian General Life

6. LAURENTIAN GROUP

Laurentian Group

Laurentian Bank
(formerly Montreal City & District)

Credit Foncier   Imperial Life

Source: *A Framework for Financial Regulation*, Economic Council, *Financial Post 500*.

Degree of Foreign Ownership and Influence

The degree of foreign influence in the deposit-accepting industry has altered substantially in the 1980s. Prior to 1980, foreign ownership in any chartered bank had been limited to less than 25 percent of the outstanding shares. Many foreign banks had established a presence in Canada, but it was confined to representative offices or investments in financial institutions other than banks.

As a result of a number of pressures, the 1980 revisions to the Bank Act permitted the entry of foreign-owned banks in a limited way. The total size of all foreign-owned banks was restricted to 8 percent of the banking sector. In addition, the foreign banks were subject to limits on branching, authorized capital, and the ratio of their borrowings to their capital. Primarily as a result of pressures from American authorities, the limit to the size of foreign banks was raised to 16 percent in early 1984. Subsequently, as discussed above, several of the foreign banks were able to grow as a result of their willingness to absorb Canadian-owned banks that were experiencing difficulties. At the end of October 1986, the 54 foreign-owned banks accounted for 12.6 percent of the Canadian dollar assets of the banking system. The addition of the assets of the two Canadian banks that have subsequently been absorbed by foreign banks raised the share of foreign banks to 16 percent of the total Canadian dollar assets.

The foreign banks have tended to emphasize specific aspects of banking activity relative to domestic banks. The most notable difference is in their reliance on the wholesale market for their funding. At the end of October 1986, when domestic banks raised 63 percent of their deposits through fixed term deposits, foreign banks depended on fixed term deposits for 96 percent of their deposits. The differences in their uses of funds are not quite as pronounced. Domestic banks held 68 percent of their assets as loans, whereas foreign banks held only 58 percent. The foreign banks, in contrast, held 18 percent of their assets in deposits with other banks, whereas domestic banks held only 11 percent with other banks.

The degree of foreign influence in the other parts of the deposit-accepting sector is very limited. Once it became possible for foreign banks to have subsidiaries in Canada, they chose to operate through this means and disposed of their ownership interests in trust and loan companies. Credit unions, as a result of their organization as co-operatives, are owned by their customers on a one member, one vote basis. Consequently, any degree of foreign influence is impossible in the credit union sector.

Industrial Organizations

Each segment of the deposit-taking industry has its own industrial organization. While the roles of these organizations differ considerably, they do perform common functions. Each serves a lobby with respect to legislation and other government actions that can affect their segment of the industry. This aspect of their activities has become especially important during the 1980s when the rules governing financial institutions have been under continual review at both the federal and provincial levels. These organizations also represent their constituents on various bodies that govern their activities. For example, representatives of the banks, trust and mortgage loan companies, and credit unions and *caisses populaires* all sit on the board of the Canadian Payments Association that governs the cheque clearing system. The organizations to varying degrees also provide educational programmes for the employees of their members. In this regard, the Canadian Bankers' Association has the largest scale of activity. Through the Institute of Canadian Bankers, it offers a variety of programmes to enhance the skills of bank employees. Finally, the organizations offer services to their member institutions. The need for these common services is greatest for the credit unions and *caisses populaires* because of the small size of the independent, local units.

The provincial centrals provide member locals with services that would be uneconomical for them to provide separately. These services include "the investment of surplus funds and the lending of funds to and conducting the clearing functions for member locals. In Canada, local credit unions are permitted to deposit their statutory liquidity reserves and other surplus funds with their centrals....They administer the online computer service which is now being introduced in many provinces" (Statistics Canada, *Financial Institutions,* p. xviii).

A third tier, or national level, exists outside Quebec in the form of the Canadian Co-operative Credit Society (CCCS). Many of its responsibilities parallel the services supplied to locals by the provincial centrals such as to "provide loans to shareholder-member organizations, provide access to external capital in support of co-operative development, and provide other financial services identified by the shareholder members...co-ordination of new products on a national basis...provision of co-ordinated support services in the areas of public relations, marketing, education and research; participation in the CPA, and participation in the evolution of international co-operative financial systems" (Statistics Canada, *Financial Institutions,* p. xix). Many of these functions, especially participation in the Canadian Payments Association, are provided to *caisses populaires* in Quebec through their provincial organization, *caisse centrale desjardins du Québec.*

Importance of the Information Revolution

The nature of the services offered by deposit-taking institutions means that the industry has been and will be very sensitive to developments in communications and information processing. Deposit-taking institutions are intimately involved in the transfer, processing and storage of information. The payments function requires the transfer of information from the payer's deposit institution to the receiver's institution; the store of value function requires the maintenance of records of customers' claims on institutions, and the lending function requires institutions to process information so as to determine the credit worthiness of their customers. The information revolution has profoundly changed the ways in which deposit-taking institutions perform their business.

The evolution of computer technology has drastically affected the record keeping function of deposit-taking institutions. The paper-based records system had severe limitations. Each branch maintained the records of its balances with its depositors and its borrowers. Branches, in turn, communicated the summary elements of their balance sheets to regional offices or head offices. Any customer was effectively limited to transacting with one or a limited number of branches at which the customer had accounts. Computer technology has permitted banks to move from paper-based to computer-based record keeping. This progression would not have been possible without parallel developments in communications technology. Deposit institutions have moved record keeping away from the branch to online computers as a result of new communications and computer technology.

In practice, new communications and information technology permeate almost every aspect of the deposit-taking industry. Table 6 lists the new technologies which chartered banks and trust companies have either introduced or plan to introduce. As can be seen, the new technology can be applied in many of the activities of the deposit-taking sector. In addition, the adoption rates for these technologies, present and planned, indicate that the deposit-taking sector will be vastly changed by the new technology. The topic of innovation and technical change will be discussed more thoroughly in chapter 7.

ROLE OF GOVERNMENT AND REGULATION

The business of deposit-taking institutions is among the most heavily regulated activities in the Canadian economy. Most of this regulation can be characterized as "prudential regulation" in that it governs the permitted activities of these institutions so as to protect the funds entrusted to them by depositors. Governments are involved in the business of deposit-taking in-

Table 6
New Technologies for Deposit-Taking Institutions

Customer Sales and Service Applications
    Automated teller machines
    Automatic cheque verification
    Pay by phone
    Automatic debit/credit systems
    "Smart" cards (with installed microprocessors)
    Home banking
    Connect to retail point of sale network
    Computerized trust management
    Computerized pension management
    Securities transfer/stockholder services

Design Technologies
    4th generation computer language

Electronic Funds Transfer (EFT)
    EFT interbranch
    EFT interbank
    EFT corporate
    EFT commercial and retail accounts

Office or Office Automation Technologies
    Mainframe/minicomputers
    Word processing
    Electronic filing
    Microcomputers/personal computers
    Internal database management systems
    Local area networks
    Computerized decision support networks
    Voice-activated computers
    Artificial intelligence/expert systems
    Integrated work stations

Telecommunications Technologies
    Private automatic branch exchange
    Electronic mail
    Voice mail
    Facsimile with built-in microprocessor
    Satellite/microwave systems
    Videotex
    Video conferencing
    Fibre optics

Source: *Ontario Task Force on Employment and Technology*, p. 28.

stitutions in two ways that are distinctly different from their involvement in other sectors of the economy. First, governments supply deposit insurance and regulate deposit-taking institutions so as to protect depositors against their failure to meet their claims. In addition, these institutions receive special regulatory treatment because of their role in the transmission of monetary policy.

Regulation

In some respects, the regulations facing different types of deposit-taking institutions are quite similar. Chartered banks, trust and mortgage loan companies, and credit unions and *caisses populaires* are all governed by rules that determine which types of assets they may hold. In contrast, the regulations governing entry differ substantially among the different types of institutions. Traditionally, it has been very difficult to establish a new bank because of high capital requirements, restrictions on ownership and, not the least, procedures involved to gain a charter. While the conditions were eased in the 1980 revision to the Bank Act, the main effect has been to encourage the entry of foreign-owned Schedule B banks. At the end of 1986, only two domestically-owned banks were operating that had not operated prior to the 1980 revisions. In total, there are only nine domestically owned banks. Entry as a trust or mortgage loan company has been easier than as a bank. The establishment of a credit union or *caisse populaire* has been easiest of all, as indicated by the 3,500 locals in existence at the end of 1986. Still, credit unions can only be organized as co-operatives.

The role of deposit-taking institutions in the transmission of monetary policy has mainly affected the chartered banks because of their predominant role as a supplier of money. The banks are influenced directly by their need to meet both cash reserve requirements and secondary reserve requirements and by their ability to borrow through lender of last resort facilities at the central bank. The chartered banks are indirectly affected by monetary policy because the main instruments of monetary policy, transfers of government deposits and open market operations, both alter the quantity of assets available to the banks to meet their reserve requirements.

Deposit Insurance

Deposit insurance was formally initiated in 1967 with the establishment of the Canada Deposit Insurance Corporation (CDIC) and the Quebec Deposit Insurance Board (QDIB). The federal government provides insurance through CDIC for deposits at banks and for most deposits at trust and mortgage loan companies, whereas provincial governments supply the insurance for deposits at credit unions and *caisses populaires* and the remaining deposits at trust and mortgage loan companies. Deposit insurance protects bank depositors against the loss of at least the first $60,000 of deposits at each institution. In practice, the effective coverage varies considerably. In the case of some recent failures, only insured deposits have been protected, whereas in other cases all deposits, whether insured or not, were guaranteed by the deposit insurer. The deposit insurer plays a special role in the regulation of deposit-taking institutions. When failure becomes imminent, the deposit insurer must decide whether to close the failing institution, arrange its merger with a healthy institution, or support its continued operation as an independent entity.

REGIONAL DISTRIBUTION OF DEPOSIT-TAKING SERVICES

Many of the activities of deposit-taking institutions have to be performed at the customer's location. The collection of retail deposits from households has been carried on traditionally through the use of local branches. Similarly, lending to consumers and small business usually requires the face-to-face access made possible through the branch. Other activities such as the collection of large deposits and lending to medium and large businesses can be more centralized at regional or even national offices.

The use of the branch for deposit collection and lending has meant that a major part of the employment offered by deposit-taking institutions has corresponded to the configuration of local offices. A number of innovations, both technical and organizational, have tended to reduce the role of the branch. The computer has permitted financial institutions to remove many record keeping functions from the branch to central locations. Moreover, the automated teller (ATM) or cash machine has reduced the customer's dependence on the local branch and its personnel for many routine banking functions. In terms of organization, many financial institutions have developed specialized personnel for activities such as lending. This specialization has tended to reduce the role of the local branch relative to regional and national offices.

Table 7 compares the regional distribution of employment and branches of deposit-taking institutions with the regional distribution of population and income. These data tend to support the view that bank services must be offered at the location of their customers. As can be seen, the pattern of employees corresponds quite closely to the provincial patterns of population and income. The most major differences are in the percentage of bank employees in Ontario and Quebec. In each case, the difference is reduced in the series for employees of all deposit-taking institutions, reflecting the greater importance of credit unions in Quebec and their lesser importance in

Table 7

Regional Distribution of Deposit-Taking Institutions, 1985

	Population	Income	Bank Branches	Credit Union Offices	Trust Companies	All Branches	Employees Bank	All
Newfoundland	2.3%	1.4%	1.9%	0.1%	1.2%	1.2%	1.2%	1.1%
Prince Edward Island	0.5	0.3	0.4	0.3	0.7	0.4	0.3	—
Nova Scotia	3.5	2.4	3.4	2.8	4.4	3.4	3.1	2.1
New Brunswick	2.8	1.8	2.5	3.4	2.2	2.7	1.8	1.8
Quebec	30.0	22.3	19.3	37.1	10.7	23.5	17.6	26.6
Ontario	35.7	38.4	38.8	28.5	53.3	36.5	46.0	38.9
Manitoba	4.2	3.8	4.8	4.7	2.7	4.5	3.9	3.6
Saskatchewan	4.0	4.0	5.4	8.8	3.2	6.3	3.4	3.4
Alberta	9.3	13.7	11.2	6.8	10.5	10.6	10.5	10.2
British Columbia	11.4	11.4	11.8	7.6	11.1	10.3	12.2	12.3

Sources: *A Framework for Financial Regulation*, Economic Council, Canadian Bankers' Association, and 1981 Census of Population.

1 m.

Demo.

Ontario. The patterns of branches diverge somewhat from population and income by province on an institution-by-institution basis, but these differences tend to disappear in the comparisons using all types of institutions.

CANADIAN INSTITUTIONS IN AN INTERNATIONAL SETTING

In recent years, trade in financial services has become an increasingly prominent element in international trade. Deposit institutions participate in foreign banking in a variety of ways, only some of which can be considered "pure" trade in financial services. A need exists to distinguish trade in financial services from financial services supplied by foreign-owned domestic banks. Trade in financial services occurs when a financial institution in one country lends to or accepts deposits from customers in another country. Financial activity by residents with a domestically-based, foreign-owned bank is considered a domestic transaction in the same way as the sale of any other product by a foreign subsidiary.

The contribution to international trade varies substantially among the different components of the deposit-taking industry. The chartered banks, on the whole, are very active in supplying banking services internationally, whereas the commitment of trust and mortgage loan companies is minor. The organization of credit unions so that they deal primarily with members virtually excludes them from international banking.

The scale of the international business of the chartered banks can be shown by examining their different types of international business (see table 8). Foreign currency liabilities, as a whole, account for $200 billion or 44.1 percent of the total liabilities of chartered banks. Some of this business cannot be considered international business in either sense in that it is booked with Canadian residents. This part totalled $12 billion or 2.6 percent of total liabilities. The business of foreign branches and subsidiaries was the largest component of foreign currency business, $103.3 billion, or over 51.1 percent of total foreign currency liabilities and 22.8 percent of total liabilities. Finally, "true" trade in financial services, foreign currency liabilities booked in Canada with non-residents, was $86.5 billion, 42.8 percent of total foreign currency liabilities and 19 percent of total liabilities.

A similar situation is revealed on the asset side. Total foreign currency assets and the division between these assets booked in Canada and booked elsewhere are virtually identical to the comparable figures on the liability side. This balance between foreign currency assets and foreign currency liabilities reflects the efforts taken by the banks to ensure that they are not exposed to the risks of foreign exchange rate changes. The only difference to be noted between their foreign exchange positions on the asset and liability sides is the

Table 8
Foreign Currency Business of the Canadian Banks
(End of August 1986)

	(in billions of dollars)
Foreign Currency Assets	
Booked in Canada	$97.6
With Canadian Residents	$35.7
With non-residents	$61.9
Booked Abroad	$104.2
Total	$201.8
Foreign Currency Liabilities	
Booked in Canada	$98.5
With Canadian Residents	$12.0
With non-residents	$86.5
Booked Abroad	$103.3
Total	$201.8

Source: *Bank of Canada Review*.

Table 9
Trade in Banking Services in Canada, 1982 to 1984

Year	Exports (billions of $)	Percentage of total exports	Percentage of service exports
1982	.68	0.7	5.7
1983	1.20	1.2	9.5
1984	.93	0.7	6.5

	Imports (billions of $)	Percentage of total imports	Percentage of service imports
1982	.74	0.9	5.7
1983	.49	0.5	2.9
1984	.54	0.5	2.9

Source: Derived from St-Hilaire and Whalley.

$23.7 billion excess of assets over liabilities booked in Canada with residents, offset almost completely by an opposite imbalance with non-residents.

The significance for Canada of the pure trade component of international banking services has been studied by St-Hilaire and Whalley, who estimate Canada's imports and exports of banking services for the years 1982, 1983, and 1984.[7] Their analysis involves two steps: the definition of trade in banking services, and the measurement of this trade on a basis equivalent to other exports and imports.

The first step was necessary because the total foreign currency business of the Canadian banks does not correspond to the basis on which trade can be measured. As seen above, some represents foreign currency business with Canadians which can be interpreted as domestic business for which the banks and their customers find it advantageous to establish contracts denominated in foreign currencies. In addition, banking operations abroad also do not constitute trade. The St-Hilaire and Whalley measures include only business booked in Canada with non-Canadians and the business of foreign banks booked abroad with Canadians as elements of foreign trade.

In the second step St-Hilaire and Whalley estimate the incomes derived from foreign trade in banking services on the same basis as other international trade. To do this, they estimate the spreads between interest rates received and paid.[8]

The St-Hilaire and Whalley estimates of trade in banking services are presented and compared with other trade statistics in table 9. As can be seen, pure trade in banking services has been quite small both absolutely and relative to total trade and trade in services. Exports of banking services accounted for only 1.2 percent of total exports and 9.5 percent of service exports in 1983, their peak year. Similarly, in their peak year (1982), banking service imports only accounted for 0.9 percent of total imports and 5.7 percent of service imports.

Canadian Banks in a World Perspective

Canadian banks are large by world standards in terms of their total assets. *The Banker,* in its survey of the 500 largest banks in the world, places five Canadian banks in the top 100: Royal, 32nd; Montreal, 40th; Commerce, 46th; Nova Scotia, 60th; and Toronto-Dominion, 75th. While Royal was approximately 40 percent of the size of the largest bank, Citicorp, four of the five largest Canadian banks would have ranked in the top ten banks in the United States, with the fifth bank ranking eleventh. To give some perspective on recent changes in world banking, none of the Canadian banks would have ranked in the top ten Japanese banks.

NOTES

1. Power and Varma (1984) list 29 separate returns that chartered banks must file in addition to the annual inspection package.

2. The remaining two Schedule A banks, the Bank of Alberta and the Western and Pacific Bank, are both very small and concentrated in Western Canada.

3. The Laurentian Group has announced that the Montreal and District Savings Bank will be applying for a Schedule B charter.

4. Tables 3 and 4 report total assets rather than just Canadian assets because this measure is most appropriate for examining the size of enterprise that characterizes the industry.

5. Two exceptions to this claim should be noted. The 1980 Bank Act introduced the possibility of the closely held Schedule B bank. In addition, chartered banks are permitted to own mortgage loan companies. These mortgage loan subsidiaries are quite large in aggregate, but are operated essentially as mortgage departments of the parent banks. Only one Canadian bank has taken the option of operating under Schedule B.

6. The *Globe and Mail* reports the following partnerships between Canadian financial institutions and securities dealers: Bank of Nova Scotia, agreement in principle to purchase 100 percent of McLeod Young Weir; Bank of Montreal, purchase of 75 percent of Wood Gundy; Canadian Imperial Bank of Commerce, $400 million joint venture company with Gordon Capital; Financial Trustco, purchase of 50 percent of Walwynn Stodgell; and Laurentian Group, owner of proposed Laurentian Bank (formerly Montreal and District Savings Bank), purchase of 23.5 percent of Geoffrion Leclerc.

7. For many activities, the importance of international trade cannot be assessed through the balance of payments statistics. These statistics do not provide a clear measure of the trade in financial services for several reasons. First, it is difficult to isolate the banking transactions from other transactions. And secondly, the balance of payments accounts mix trade items such as interest earned and paid on intermediation with income from investments such as profits earned by foreign branches. See Statistics Canada (1981).

8. This procedure will omit any income earned through service charges.

Chapter 3

OUTPUT AND PRODUCTIVITY IN THE DEPOSIT-TAKING SECTOR

MEASUREMENT OF FINANCIAL SECTOR OUTPUT: CONCEPTUAL PROBLEMS

The measurement of the output of the financial sector poses a special set of problems for this study because the present methods have been continually subject to controversy. In particular, the application of the conventions of national income as used for other industries would produce, if rigorously applied, a negative measure of output for the financial sector. This apparent anomaly has led national income accountants to use a so-called imputation in the measurement of the output of the financial sector. A first step in any quantitative analysis of the size, growth and productivity of the financial sector must be understanding the problems involved in these measurements.

CURRENT APPROACH TO MEASUREMENT

The measurement of the output of the financial sector takes place within the context of a system of measurement for the output of the economy as a whole. This system is known as the Canadian System of National Accounts. Ruggles and Ruggles (1982), in their discussion of the U.S. accounts, suggest that "it is now generally recognized that national accounts have three major functions. They serve as the coordinating and integrating framework for all economic statistics; they give timely and reliable key indicators on the performance of the economy; and they illuminate the relationships among the sectors of the economy that are fundamental to its functioning" (p. 1).

This study of the financial sector as a service industry focuses on the latter function. It reviews the relations of the financial sector with the rest of the economy: the uses of its outputs, its use of inputs from other sectors, and the changes in these relationships. From this perspective, the measurement of the output of the financial sector must reflect as closely as possible the same principles that are used to measure the output of other sectors in the economy.

VALUE-ADDED APPROACH

The value-added approach to the calculation of national income measures the output of any sector by the sum of payments that it makes for productive inputs. These payments include wages and salaries, rent, interest and profit. Any payments to other firms for their products are not included and are treated as payments for intermediate inputs. The use of the value-added approach avoids double counting in the contribution of different enterprises in the production of final output and permits a unique identification of the contribution of each stage to the final product.

A number of complications arise from trying to apply the value-added approach, especially in the treatment of interest payments. A problem arises with interest payments because some firms receive interest payments from some sources while making interest payments to others. The interest received by the firm will have already counted as part of value added of another enterprise. Thus, it would lead to inappropriate double counting to include that part of interest again as an element of value added. The national income accountants have established a convention that any interest received by a firm be deducted from its interest payments in reaching a measure of its value added so as to eliminate any double counting from this source.

IMPUTATION FOR FINANCIAL INSTITUTIONS

While the convention adopted for interest provides a consistent treatment for typical enterprises, it creates a severe problem when applied to financial institutions whose primary business involves borrowing funds from one group and lending to another. Consistent application of the interest convention to financial institutions will typically result in very small or negative value added for these firms. Thus, it is argued that the conventional methods for measuring value added cannot be applied to banks and other financial institutions.

Table 10 shows a hypothetical example of the income and product originating in banking that illustrates the difficulties in applying the national income conventions to the financial sector. The problem arises on the income side because the intermediary receives 1,200 in interest and only pays 550. The interest element alone contributes -650 to value added, an amount that in this case more than offsets the other elements and leads to a negative value added. Similarly, on the product side, the deposit-taking firm purchases 200

Table 10

Conventional Measures of Income and Product Applied to Banking

	(in millions of dollars)
Income earned in deposit-taking sector	
Wages and salaries paid	350
Net interest paid	−650
Monetary interest paid	(550)
Less	
Interest received	(−1200)
Profits	250
Income originating	−50
Product of deposit-taking sector	
Service charges	150
Less	
Current purchases from other firms	200
Product originating	−50

Source: Statistics Canada, 13-549E.

Table 11

Imputed Measures of Income and Product in Banking

	(In millions of dollars)
Income	
Wages and salaries paid	350
Net interest paid	0
Monetary interest paid	(550)
Imputed interest paid	(650)
Less	
Interest received	(−1200)
Profits	250
Income originating	600
Product	
Service charges	800
Monetary	(150)
Imputed	(650)
Less	
Current purchases from other firms	200
Product originating	600

Source: Statistics Canada, 13-549E.

from other firms that more than offsets the 150 revenue that it gains from service charges.

A negative value added for a sector performing an economic service is clearly an unacceptable outcome. The national accounts overcome this problem by incorporating an "imputation" of additional interest paid on the income account that is equal to the difference between the interest paid and the interest received by financial institutions. An equal imputation of service charges is made on the product side. In effect, this imputation treats the financial firms as if they distribute all the interest they receive as interest payments to their customers and then collect a service charge equal to the difference between interest paid and interest received. Table 11 shows that the imputation causes the value added in the financial sector to always equal the sum of factor payments other than interest.

A final feature of the present approach for measuring the output of financial institutions consists of the allocation of the value added of financial institutions on the expenditure side of the accounts. Statistics Canada reports that

> the domestic portion of this total applicable to depositors is then allocated between persons, governments, and corporations on the basis of the deposit holdings of each group. By far the greatest part of the imputation—about four fifths of it—is applicable to persons, and the amount is included in "interest, dividends and miscellaneous investment income" paid out to persons by the corporate and business enterprises sector. A relatively small amount is applicable to government, and this is included in "profits remitted by government business enterprises," in the outlay side of the corporate and government business enterprises sector account. The remainder of the imputation is applicable to corporations; since intra-corporate transactions cancel out, this amount is not explicitly included in the income or outlay account of this sector (13-549E, p. 202).

Statistics Canada goes on to state in a footnote that "financial institutions also provide some 'free' services to borrowers, and an imputation for these services is also incorporated in the calculations" (13-549E, p. 202). Thus, through the imputation, Statistics Canada is able to allocate the imputed output of financial institutions among different final and intermediate uses in a similar manner to other outputs in the economy.

Desired Features of Any Measure of the Financial Sector

The imputation used for the measure of value added for financial institutions has been severely criticized on a number of grounds with many of the critics of the imputation proposing their own alternative approaches. The weaknesses and strengths of the present method and its alternatives should be assessed as a precondition to any quantitative analysis of the financial sector. If the present approach is adopted, at least its limitations will be understood. Alternatively, another approach can be adopted if the limitations of the present imputation appear to be too severe. Any comparison of alternative measures of financial sector output must be based on understood criteria. The remainder of this section discusses the following important criteria: the treatment of capital to reflect the production structure, the treatment of like transactions in a similar manner independent of the form of intermediation, and the use of an acceptable approach to imputation. Each of these criteria is discussed more fully below.

Treatment of Capital

A major question with respect to the present treatment of capital concerns interest payments that are made by one enterprise to another. In the present practice, interest is considered as a factor payment only at the first stage in the sequence of transactions. Payments of interest by enterprises further along in the chain of payments are treated so as to have the interest receipts of these enterprises netted against them to avoid double counting. This procedure for the avoidance of double counting creates the need for the imputation for the value added for financial institutions. This treatment of interest identifies the payment of capital services with the enterprise at which these capital services are used. The procedure thus attempts to reflect the production structure of the economy.

The present procedure captures the production structure by recording the payment for capital services by the sector that uses the capital. If equity funds finance the capital, the income is treated as profit; if debt finances the capital, the income is treated as interest. This approach ensures that the payment of capital services will be measured the same regardless of the form of finance. By doing so, this procedure estimates production arrangements consistently on the basis of factor incomes.

The way in which the present procedures illuminate the structure of production can be seen from considering an example of two different production structures. In one case, a sandwich maker produces both sandwiches and the bread from which the sandwiches are made. In the other case, the sandwich maker makes sandwiches from purchased bread. In both cases, the sandwich makers finance their equipment by borrowing from a venture capital firm that, in turn, finances itself by borrowing from the general public.

The existing procedures for the treatment of interest payments clearly reflect the difference in the production structure of the two firms. The first firm makes interest payments for the services gained from capital in both processes, the production of sandwiches and the production of bread. In contrast, the other manufacturer makes interest payments for the capital services required for the production of sandwiches and purchases the intermediate product, bread, from a baker. The baker, in turn, makes interest payments for the capital services required to produce bread. The national accounts, as currently presented, make a clear differentiation among these two structures of production. They indicate that more capital is used in producing sandwiches and bread than is required for producing sandwiches from purchased bread.

Organization of the Financial Sector

The process of intermediation can be organized in a variety of ways. It may occur through deposit intermediaries (financial institutions) or through market intermediaries (brokers). The basis on which choice is made, though imperfectly understood, depends on the need for and comparative advantages in the supply and assessment of information and the supervision of ultimate borrowers. In some cases, the margin of choice between the alternative forms of intermediation may be very narrow, whereas it may be more substantial in others. Nevertheless, in many cases, marked differences of form among intermediaries may have little significance with respect to the processes performed by these intermediaries and their economic importance. To the extent that similar services are performed in apparently different forms, they should be treated in a like manner in the national accounts.

A problem arises for national accounting because of the differences among intermediaries in the way that they charge for their services. The form of payment for market intermediaries is relatively uncomplicated. They generally charge an explicit fee for their services. In contrast, the payments to financial intermediaries is much more complex. Sometimes they charge an explicit fee which constitutes the total payment for their services; at other times, they are paid through the spread between their lending and borrowing rates. Still these differences need not reflect any essential difference in the nature of the economic services supplied. As a consequence, it seems desirable that the method adopted to measure the output of intermediaries avoid differences in measurement that arise solely from different pricing practices that have little economic significance.

The Principle of Imputation

As already discussed, the present methods of national income accounting require the use of an imputation to produce a measure of the value added for financial institutions. This imputation is required because of the present treatment of interest in the national accounts. Any change in the approach to the measurement of national income would create different problems for the measurement of the financial sector. The nature of the imputation would depend on the system of national accounts adopted. Given the pricing practices of the financial sector, some form of imputation seems unavoidable. Nevertheless, the above-mentioned standards should be met by any system of imputation that is chosen.

Need for Imputation

Serious conceptual concerns about the treatment of the financial sector in the national accounts have been raised in a series of articles by two Canadian scholars: Rymes (1985, 1986) and Sunga (1967, 1984). Each offers his own interpretation of the need for the imputation. Rymes suggests that the imputation arises from the effects of regulation, in particular the minimum cash reserve requirement, on the pricing used by financial institutions. Sunga attributes the imputation to the peculiarities in the treatment of capital income in the national accounts. Neither of these arguments appears to be sufficient to explain the need for imputation. The treatment of capital income would not matter if financial institutions made explicit charges for their services. Similarly, as will be shown, the use of spreads by financial institutions to gain their revenues need not cause the problems of the present imputation under some alternative treatments of interest income. The imputation problem exists because the pricing practices adopted by financial institutions generate problems when combined with the conventions adopted for the treatment of capital income.

The imputation problem arises on the income side of the national accounts because payments are traced backward from the final producer to the ultimate receiver of the income. The procedure used for capital income attributes all the payments of capital income made by the final producer as the income of the immediate recipient of that payment regardless of any payments of capital income that the recipient makes to others. As a consequence, any counting of further interest payments at lower stages of the production chain would be an inappropriate double counting. The deduction of interest receipts from interest payments is the device by which this double counting is avoided.

The source of the imputation problem can be seen by examining why a parallel problem does not arise when similar pricing practices are adopted by retailers. Retailers gain their margin by adding a mark-up to their factor costs and their payments for intermediate goods. An imputation is not required because the payments are less than the revenues gained from the sale of the output, leaving a residual that is attributed to the activity of merchandising. The forward approach to measurement of output used here avoids the imputation problem because the measurement proceeds forward from the lowest level of production to the final stages of production. By moving forward, this approach only counts the additions to the value of output that occur in each successive stage of production.

THE FLOW-THROUGH APPROACH

The "flow-through" approach is proposed as a method for measuring the value added of the financial sector.[1] It is argued that the flow-through approach offers a clearer justification for the imputation for much of the output of the financial sector and is consistent with the criteria developed earlier in this chapter. This approach represents a logical modification to the present treatment of interest in the national accounts. Any interest payment by the productive sector where the interest payment is made directly to the ultimate lenders would be treated the same as at present. The productive enterprise makes an income payment, and an ultimate lender earns an income. The difference arises when an enterprise in the productive sector makes an interest payment to another enterprise that in turn makes interest payments to an ultimate lender. That element of the original interest payment that is paid by the intermediate enterprise would be treated as if it were paid directly from the productive enterprise to the ultimate lender. It is an income payment by the productive sector and an income receipt of the ultimate lender. In this sense, it is passed through the intermediate stage. The remainder of the interest paid by the productive enterprise equals the spread between the interest received and the interest paid by the intermediary. This part represents the income payments of the intermediary and, as under the current imputation, is treated as the value added of the intermediary. Unlike the current treatment, it is not counted as an income payment by the productive sector. In multi-stage transaction chains, the procedure is repeated at each stage. Only the interest receipts of the ultimate lenders in the chain are treated as income payments by the productive sector. The spread between the interest paid and received at each stage in the chain is treated as the value added of that part of the chain.[2]

The earlier discussion outlined criteria which an acceptable measure of the value added of the financial sector should meet. Each will be reviewed in turn.

Treatment of Capital Income

The most significant difference between the present and proposed approaches arises with respect to part of the interest payments made by the production sector. The flow-through approach treats the part that is passed through the intermediaries and treated as income received by ultimate lenders and income payments by productive enterprises exactly the same as under the present method. The difference arises with respect to the remainder of the interest payments made by the productive sector, the part that is the spread between the interest received and paid by intermediaries. The flow-through approach, by treating the spreads as a payment for monitoring and supervisory services, assigns them as the income of the intermediaries. The current approach attributes all these payments as net interest, a treatment that is inconsistent with the modern theory of financial intermediation.

National income accountants stress the need for the payment for capital services to be attributed to the production sector that uses the capital. The flow-through approach achieves this objective, though with a different emphasis than the current approach. Only part of the interest paid by the productive sector is viewed as a payment for capital services. Pure payments for the services of capital are recognized as a factor payment by the production sector and as income by the recipients. These payments are passed through the financial sector without affecting its value added. This treatment is perfectly consistent with the objective of identifying payments for capital services with the production sector. The difference arises with respect to the remainder of the interest payments attributed to the productive sector, that part that is the counterpart to the interest spread of the intermediaries. Unlike the current practice, the proposal treats these as the value added of the intermediaries rather than value added of the productive enterprises. From a practical standpoint, the current measures of value added for deposit-taking institutions remain valid; only their justification is changed.

Organization of the Financial Sector

A desirable measure should avoid differences in the measurement of the income of financial intermediaries and market intermediaries and avoid differences in measurement as a result of different methods of payment for the services of intermediaries. By keeping the payment for intermediation separate from the payment for the services of capital, the flow-through approach eliminates the differences in treatment of market and financial intermediaries. Both have their own value added derived without the need for an imputation. Moreover, for financial intermediaries, the measurement will be the same whether the intermediary is paid explicitly through service charges or implicitly through a spread between its lending and borrowing rates. In both cases, there is a payment for the services of capital that is attributed to the direct lenders and a separate payment for the services of intermediaries.

The Principle of Imputation

As suggested earlier, any measure of value added in the financial sector should be consistent with the approach applied to other sectors. The flow-through approach gives the same measure of value added for the financial sector as the present imputation. Nevertheless, its conceptual basis is entirely different. In the flow-through approach, only part of the interest paid by the production sector is treated as a payment for the services of capital. The remainder becomes a payment for the supervisory services of intermediaries and is treated as part of the income of the financial sector. As with other sectors, the value added for the financial sector equals the sum of its payments for productive services. From a practical standpoint, the current measures of value added for the financial sector remain valid; only their justification is changed.

MEASUREMENT OF INCOME

The present approach to measurement of the value added for the financial sector has been subject to continual questioning. It is often argued that the imputation used for this sector is inconsistent with the methods used for other sectors. The objectives of the national accounts as applied to the financial sector have been explored in some detail so as to gain a greater appreciation of the issues at stake. A flow-through approach has been proposed as a means for achieving the objective of a consistent and defensible measure of the value added in the financial sector. This approach has been found to satisfy the criteria for a measure of the output of the financial sector that were proposed earlier. Interestingly enough, the flow-through approach does not require a massive restructuring of the national accounts of the financial sector. Rather, it supplies a sounder and more consistent justification for current methods of measurement.

A PRACTICAL PROBLEM IN OUTPUT COMPARISONS

The measurement of output of the deposit-taking sector by an imputation equal to the spread between interest received and interest paid by deposit-taking institutions causes practical problems for the comparison of output on a year-to-year basis. The interest rates received and paid by financial institutions are the outcome of a variety of different contracts that reflect the preferences of both lenders and borrowers. Some contracts, such as some bonds, have their interest terms fixed for long periods of time, whereas others are adjusted frequently in line with market rates. Thus, the spread earned by deposit-taking institutions at any time may have been determined by the patterns of interest rates that have existed in the past. In a static world, the imputation would capture the amounts that lenders would pay to avoid having to lend directly to the ultimate borrowers on the same terms as the deposit-taking institutions do. They are willing to give up some return to avoid the risks, administrative costs and supervision that are borne by the deposit-taking institutions. The imputation as measured by the interest spread would be an accurate measure of the services of intermediaries in this static world.

Other factors enter into the determination of spreads in a dynamic world. The interest rate spread at any time is determined by the recent history of interest rates and the maturities chosen by the intermediaries and their customers in making deposit and loan contracts.[3]

Suppose, for example, that interest rates on deposits were set for two years and that interest rates on loans were continually adjusted to market rates. If the general level of interest rates remained stable, the spread earned by intermediaries would reflect the difference between two-year interest rates and short interest rates. Part of the spread would measure the compensation to the intermediaries bearing the risks of interest rate changes.

The spread earned by an intermediary would rise if interest rates rose over the two years and would fall if interest rates fell. The intermediaries' spreads move with market interest rates because the deposit side of the contract is fixed, whereas the loan side is tied to market rates. The intermediaries' spread would move in the opposite direction to market rates if the loan side were fixed and the deposit side responded to market rates.

What significance do these movements in spreads have for the measurement of output in the deposit-taking sector? Do movements in these spreads in response to market rates reflect real changes in the output of intermediaries? It is difficult to see that any change has occurred in the services supplied by intermediaries. Moreover, new business is likely to be conducted on the same terms unless the perception of the risks and other costs of lending have been changed. All that has happened is that one of the risks that banks undertake, a change in market interest rates, has taken place.

The argument to this point suggests that the spreads realized by deposit-taking institutions includes two elements: the spread that borrowers and lenders pay to conduct their business through an intermediary, and the change in the original spread caused by subsequent movements in interest rates. Conceptually, the appropriate method for measuring the value that customers place on the services of intermediaries requires consideration of only the first element. Ideally, this approach would examine the *ex ante* or intended spreads as distinct from the *ex post* or realized spreads that are actually observed.[4]

This criticism suggests that care should be taken in interpreting output and productivity changes for the deposit-taking sector on a year-to-year basis. Such changes can reflect the movements of the general level of interest rates. This argument suggests that productivity changes should be measured over relatively long periods of time over which fixed contracts will have worked their way through to maturity. Alternatively, short run changes in productivity should be treated with caution.

THE MEASUREMENT OF REAL OUTPUT

The discussion to this point has focused on the measurement of the value added of the financial sector. Value added measures the money value of the output which is composed of two elements: the real value of output, and the price of that output. The measurement of the real output of the financial sector poses similar problems to those in the measurement of its value added. Unlike the case of goods and even many service producing industries, a problem exists in defining the output of financial institutions.

The earlier discussion in chapter 2 suggested that financial institutions supply a wide variety of closely related services that include the transfer of payments and the management and supervision of portfolios of loans and securities. The quantification of these services faces difficulty in the same sense of the quantification of good health supplied by medical services. In the measurement of health services, this problem is overcome by measuring instead the variety of actions and procedures that are performed by the health services industry. The same procedures are used in measuring the real output of the financial sector. Financial services are broken down into their component operations and an index of these components is used to measure output. Division of this index into the imputed income of the deposit-taking sector gives a price index for the services of the financial sector.

OUTPUT IN THE DEPOSIT-TAKING SECTOR

Output at Current Prices

Table 12 shows the gross domestic product (GDP) at current prices of both the deposit-taking sector and the larger finance, insurance and real estate sector relative to the GDP of the service industry and overall GDP for the period 1973-83. The data as shown in figure 1 provide an indication of the importance of the deposit-taking sector in the economy over time. At the beginning of the period in 1973, the deposit-taking sector accounted for 1.6 percent of total GDP. Over the immediately subsequent years, the product of this sector grew faster than the rest of the economy so that by 1977 it accounted for al-

Table 12

Estimates of Output in Current Prices

	1971	1972	1973	1974	1975	1976	1977	1978	1979	1980	1981	1982	1983
Banks and Other Deposit-Accepting Establishments													
Gross output	1860.4	2141.1	2544.8	3137.6	3935.5	4520.9	5135.6	5678.4	6016.6	6836.0	7884.4	8836.0	10308.4
Intermediate inputs	587.8	722.2	826.3	1016.9	1220.7	1467.3	1615.4	1879.6	2104.3	2673.3	3327.7	3701.9	4329.8
Gross domestic product	1272.6	1418.9	1718.5	2120.7	2714.8	3053.6	3520.2	3798.8	3912.3	4162.7	4556.7	5143.1	5978.6
Finance, Insurance and Real Estate													
Gross output	16487.6	18097.8	20919.5	25030.5	29550.1	34622.4	39310.8	44815.0	50512.6	57845.9	64998.1	72135.2	80915.3
Intermediate inputs	6898.5	7745.3	8828.7	10209.1	12260.0	14157.2	15859.3	17421.1	19595.0	22560.3	26166.4	28500.6	31338.0
Gross domestic product	9588.9	10352.4	12090.9	14821.2	17240.0	20465.2	23451.5	27393.9	30917.6	35285.6	38831.7	43634.6	49577.3
Service industry output			63303.7	75844.4	88718.1	103394.7	113760.5	127844.8	143614.0	162136.6	183010.0	200510.9	220925.1
Gross domestic product			109921.6	132000.3	148769.9	171034.8	187818.7	210838.0	242550.3	271922.6	304617.8	319057.0	351039.4
GDP of Deposit-Accepting Institutions As a Percentage of													
GDP of financial services			0.1421	0.1431	0.1575	0.1492	0.1501	0.1387	0.1265	0.1180	0.1173	0.1179	0.1206
GDP of all services			0.0271	0.0280	0.0306	0.0295	0.0309	0.0297	0.0272	0.0257	0.0249	0.0256	0.0271
Overall GDP			0.0156	0.0161	0.0182	0.0179	0.0187	0.0180	0.0161	0.0153	0.0150	0.0161	0.0170

Source: Statistics Canada, Gross Domestic Product by Industry, 61-005.

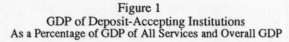

Figure 1
GDP of Deposit-Accepting Institutions
As a Percentage of GDP of All Services and Overall GDP

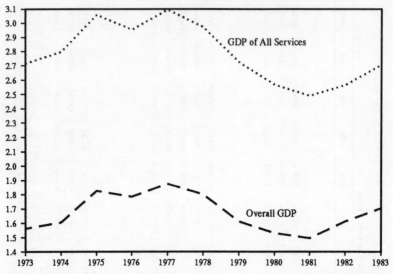

most 1.9 percent of overall domestic product. From then on the GDP of the deposit-taking sector as a share of overall domestic product declined to a level of only 1.5 percent in 1981 before recovering to 1.7 percent in 1983. Thus, despite fluctuations over the period, the share of gross domestic product originating from the deposit-taking sector had grown by roughly 10 percent over the decade. The growth rate of real GDP for the sector was 13.3 percent a year compared to the 12.3 percent growth for GDP overall over the years 1973 to 1983.

A similar pattern without the trend is shown in the comparison of the deposit-taking sector and service industries as a whole (also presented in figure 1). After starting at 2.7 percent, the share of the deposit-taking sector in the service sector reached its maximum of almost 3.1. percent in 1977, declined to a low of 2.5 percent in 1981, and recovered to its initial level of 2.7 percent in 1983.

Much caution must be used in interpreting these movements of the deposit-taking sector relative to other sectors and the economy as a whole. As already discussed, the movements in the output of the deposit-taking sector are affected by the interaction of interest rates with the contract structure of the sector's assets and liabilities. The period under review was characterized by substantial volatility of interest rates and induced adjustments in the terms of many financial contracts. Given the size of the interest swings from year to year, not too much significance should be attached to annual changes in the share. Similarly, though the data suggest a trend over the period, the same factors together with the importance of the choice of the final period in determining the trend give little confidence that the trend reflects a real sustained phenomenon.

Implicit Prices

The movements in output of the deposit-taking sector at current prices could be caused by movements in real output or in the price level of the services produced by the sector. Table 13, showing the movements of the implicit price for the deposit-taking sector relative to the implicit price index for GDP, indicates that the prices for deposit-taking services moved quite differently than prices for all output over the period. Initially, the price index for the deposit-taking sector increased so that by 1975 it had become 10 percent higher than its initial level relative to the GDP deflator. Over the next six years, the trend was reversed, and the price index for the deposit-taking sector declined sharply relative to the GDP deflator, reaching a level in 1981 that was 76 percent of its initial level and 70 percent of its 1975 peak. The downward relative trend in the deflator for the deposit-taking sector was reversed in 1982 and 1983, with a sharp rise relative to the GDP deflator in 1983. Over the period, the price deflator for the deposit-taking sector grew at 9.2 percent compared to 9.8 percent for the GDP deflator for the economy. By the end of the period, the deflator was 94 percent of its original level relative to the GDP deflator. The movements of the last two years suggest that the causes of the trend may have abated. In these years alone, over three-quarters of the relative decrease in the deflator up to 1981 was reversed.

Real Output

The real GDP of the deposit-taking sector, as shown in table 14, stood at 1.7 percent of overall real GDP. Over the next decade, this proportion increased in every year except two, 1980 and 1983. By the end of the period, the real output in the deposit-taking sector had grown to almost 2 percent of overall output, almost a 16 percent increase in its share. As in the case of the price deflator, the trend was reversed in the last two years of the period. Though the reversal was less dramatic, it offset roughly one-third of the peak share of real GDP realized by the deposit-taking sector in 1981. Over the whole period, real GDP in the deposit-taking sector grew at 3.8 percent compared to the 2.2 percent for GDP overall.

Table 13

Implicit Price Indexes for the Deposit-Taking Sector and GDP, 1973-83

Implicit Price Index	1973	1974	1975	1976	1977	1978	1979	1980	1981	1982	1983	Growth Rate
1. Gross domestic product	116	133	148	162	173	188	209	231	252	275	295	0.098
2. GDP of deposit-taking	106	123	149	151	157	165	161	171	276	203	255	0.092
Ratio 2/1	0.914	0.925	1.007	0.932	0.908	0.878	0.770	0.740	1.095	0.738	0.864	-0.006

Source: Same as table 12.

Table 14

Real Gross Domestic Product for the Deposit-Taking Sector and GDP, 1973-83

Gross Domestic Product	1973	1974	1975	1976	1977	1978	1979	1980	1981	1982	1983	Growth Rate
1. Economy	95028	99347	100283	105416	108329	111879	116296	117780	121053	115888	118983	0.023
2. Deposit-Taking	1616	1720	1816	2027	2236	2308	2433	2440	2586	2535	2400	0.040
Ratio 2/1	0.017	0.017	0.018	0.019	0.021	0.021	0.021	0.021	0.021	0.022	0.020	0.017

Source: Same as table 12.

SUMMARY

The measurement of the output of the deposit-taking sector poses a number of conceptual difficulties. Rigid adherence to the conventions of national income accounting for this sector would cause its output to be negative or very small. A much criticized imputation has been used to provide a measure of the sector's output. An examination of the rationale for the imputation suggests that this rationale does not adequately portray the function of financial intermediaries. A modified rationale based on the flow-through approach recognizes the role of intermediaries and, surprisingly, gives a stronger justification for the present imputation.

Examination of the measures of output for the deposit-taking sector suggest that its experience was distinctly different from the economy as a whole. While the overall trend in GDP in current prices did not differ too much from the trend of GDP, the price deflator fell at roughly 0.6 percent per year relative to the overall GDP deflator. As a result, the deposit-taking sector grew considerably more vigorously than the overall economy, with a real growth rate of 3.8 percent relative to 2.2 percent for real GDP.

NOTES

1. The "flow through" is named after the tax arrangements by which certain tax benefits accruing from investments are, passed through mutual funds to the ultimate investor.

2. Since the flow-through approach gives the same measure of output as the present approach, the allocation of the output of the financial sectors among final demands and intermediate outputs can remain unchanged.

3. These problems would not be appreciably different if financial institutions levied explicit service charges. Lenders would receive and borrowers would pay some "pure" interest rate that could in some circumstances be fixed for the period of the contract. Movements in interest rates would cause a spread to develop between borrowing and lending rates whenever the financial institution failed to maintain a balance between the maturities of its assets and liabilities.

4. The argument suggests that there is a minimum period over which the income of financial intermediaries should be measured. From the perspective of interest rate movements, this period should be long enough so that unexpected movements can be reflected in contracts. This need for an appropriate period of measurement is not unique to financial institutions. Obviously, the day, the week, the month, or even the year may not be adequate for measuring household income.

Chapter 4

EMPLOYMENT AND EARNINGS IN THE DEPOSIT-TAKING SECTOR

EMPLOYMENT IN THE INDUSTRY

Availability of Data

Table 15, summarizing the statistics for employment in the deposit-taking sector during the period 1960-86, shows that the availability of data varies greatly among the elements of the financial sector. Employment data for the entire sector represented by SIC 701 are available only for the years 1983 and following. Two series, one broader and one narrower than the deposit-taking industry, are available for the entire period 1960 to 1986. The broader series consists of the aggregate for financial institutions (SIC 701-707 for the 1970 classification). Unfortunately, this broader series has a change in coverage between 1982 and 1983 which limits the comparisons that can be made. The narrower series, supplied by the Canadian Bankers' Association, shows employment in the chartered banks and appears to have been presented on a relatively consistent basis throughout the entire period. In addition to these longer series, data are available for employment in trust and loans companies for 1973 onward, and savings and credit institutions (SIC 701-703) for 1978 onward.[1]

Table 15

Data on Employment in Deposit-Taking Sector

Series	Sector	Employment	Employment as % of SIC 701
SIC 701-07	Financial Institutions	303,800	125
SIC 701-03	Savings and Credit Institutions	259,400	107
SIC 701	Deposit Accepting	242,000	100
	Chartered Banks	162,163	67

Sources: Statistics Canada, 72-002 and Canadian Bankers Association, "Trends in Employment, Canada's Chartered Banks," May 31, 1984.

The significance of the lack of data for the deposit-accepting sector for the entire period depends on the degree to which the available measures can represent the sector. On the basis of the 1985 data, the available series are compared in table 15. The broader, long running series "financial institutions" included only 25 percent more employment than the target industry in 1985, whereas the narrow, long running series "chartered banks" covers two-thirds of the employment in the deposit-accepting institutions, the target sector.

A further perspective on the usefulness of the two longer series can be gained from comparing their relation to each other over the period. At the beginning of the period in 1960, employment in the chartered banks comprised 71 percent of the total employment of the broader aggregate, financial institutions. By 1982, the last year before the break in coverage in the broader series, the share of the banks had shrunk to only 62.5 percent. These comparisons suggest that the conclusions drawn from the available longer series, though not strictly accurate, will be broadly representative of the deposit-accepting sector as a whole. Still, care will be taken to indicate the differences that are apparent in the different categories.

Growth in Employment

The various measures of growth in employment in the financial sector over the period 1960-86 in table 16 show a slightly different pattern for each of the elements of the industry. Consider first the two longer series, financial institutions and the chartered banks, over the period in which strict comparisons are possible. The broader aggregate, employment in financial institutions (initially 702-704 and later 701-707) expanded continually throughout the period, reaching a level in 1982 that was 2.6 times its level in 1960. Similarly, the narrower aggregate, employment in chartered banks, increased by 1982 to a level that was 2.3 times its level in 1962. On an annual basis, employment in financial institutions grew at a rate of 4.4 percent over the period, while employment in banks grew at 3.9 percent.

The two series exhibit different behaviour over five-year subperiods. From 1960 to 1965, employment in financial institutions expanded by 31.5 percent, whereas employment in banks grew by only 17 percent. The difference between the growth rates was slight between 1965 and 1970 when the financial institutions grew by 23 percent and the banks by 21 percent. The years from 1970 to 1975 represent the only period in which the banks, growing by 41 percent, expanded faster than financial institutions, which nevertheless grew at 28 percent. In the final period of comparable data, financial institutions expanded their employment by 26 percent and banks by 17 percent.

Table 16

Employment in Financial Institutions, Various Measures, 1960-1986

	I 702-704 Financial Institutions	II 702 Savings and Credit Institutions	III 701 Deposit-Accepting Institutions	IV Chartered Banks	V Trust and Loan Companies	VI 031-899 Industrial Composite	VII I/VI	VIII II/VI	IX IV/VI
1960	91110			64757		2866502	0.032		0.023
1965	119884			75728		3367620	0.036		0.022
1970	147711			91597		3751591	0.039		0.024
1975	188700			129027	17421	4297400	0.044		0.030
1976	196600			137143	18982	4298300	0.046		0.032
1977	211300			146930	20197	4295200	0.049		0.034
1978	221200	203400		151064	22025	4316600	0.051	0.047	0.035
1979	235300	214600		155714	22188	4709600	0.050	0.046	0.033
1980	237200	216500		151140	27849	4664200	0.051	0.046	0.032
1981	242200	217700		155955	28387	4814100	0.050	0.045	0.032
1982	245400	221500		153433	26491	4557200	0.054	0.049	0.034
1983	281700	239600	220900.000	148184	27761	4661000 / 8661000	0.033	0.028	0.017
1984	288200	239900	221000.000	146746		8877900	0.032	0.027	0.017
1985	303800	259400	242000.000	162163		9189200	0.033	0.028	0.018
1986	315600	268900	252500.000	161712		9368500	0.034	0.029	0.017

Sources: I, II, III and VI, Statistics Canada, 72-002, larger firm data for 1960 to 1982 and firms of all sizes for 1983 to 1985.
IV, Canadian Bankers Association, "Trends in Employment, Canada's Chartered Banks," May 31, 1984.
VI, Trust Companies Association of Canada.

These differences in the growth rates of employment between the two measures correspond to what might be expected as the result of the changes in the regulatory environment facing the different institutions. In the 1960 to 1965 subperiod with rising interest rates, the banks were beginning to experience the constraining effects of the 6 percent ceiling to the interest rate that they were permitted to charge on loans. Other financial institutions that were not subject to these ceilings were able to increase their market share at the expense of the banks. The next period, 1965 to 1970, was mixed in that the interest ceiling on the banks was removed part way through the period. As a consequence, the growth of the banks was comparable to the growth of other financial institutions. This pattern reversed itself from 1970 to 1975 when the banks were totally free of the interest ceiling and outgrew other financial institutions by 41 percent to 28 percent.

The employment experience in the 1980s was distinctly different from the other subperiods. Whereas employment had expanded substantially in all sectors of the financial sector from 1960 to 1980, a very different pattern emerged in the 1980s when employment growth slowed substantially and in some cases halted. The chartered banks, the most prominent example, reached an employment level of 155,714 in 1979, maintained the same level over the next two years, and then declined steadily to a level of 146,746, almost 6 percent lower, in 1984. A similar, though slightly less pronounced, pattern also occurred for the trust and loan companies. Employment in this sector reached its peak of 28,387 in 1981, two years later than the peak in banking. This pattern did not emerge, however, in the data presented for the different levels of SIC aggregates for the financial industry. Employment expanded every year from 1979 to 1985 (excluding the 1982-83 comparison because of lack of comparability).

The difference between the two sets of employment data over the 1980s appears to reflect the treatment of part-time employment. As discussed above, the faster growing SIC data includes all workers whereas the data for the chartered banks and the trust and loan companies include only full-time workers. The importance of this difference in explaining the dissimilar trends in the series can be assessed by using figures reported by the Canadian Bankers' Association (CBA) on both regular part-time employees (head count and full-time equivalence) and all part-time employees (full-time equivalence) for the years 1981 and 1984. The CBA reports 15,478 regular part-time employees in 1981, and 22,305 in 1984. The addition of these part-time workers changes the CBAs total employment in banking from 155,955 to 171,433 in 1981, and from 146,746 to 169,051 in 1984. This change alone, though not eliminating the decrease in employment, reduces it from over 9,200 to 2,300.

Comparison of the full-time equivalence of regular part-time and all part-time employees suggests that the inclusion of temporary part-time employees would probably eliminate the rest of the apparent decline in employment in banking. Between 1981 and 1984, part-time workers as a whole increased from 11,907 to 18,495 full-time equivalent workers. At the same time, regular part-time workers increased from 7,009 to 10,979 full-time equivalents. These figures indicate that temporary part-time workers increased by 2,618, from 4,898 to 7,516 full-time equivalents. This correction for temporary part-time workers suggests that employment on a full-time equivalent worker basis did not decline over the period from 1981 to 1984.

Employment as a Percentage of Industrial Employment

Employment in the deposit-taking sector grew relative to the employment in industry as a whole. In 1960, financial institutions accounted for 3.2 percent of industrial employment and the banks for 2.3 percent. Employment in financial institutions as a group increased in every subperiod from 1960 to 1980 and appears to have increased steadily through the 1980s. Over the period covered, financial institutions virtually doubled their share of industrial employment. A similar, but less pronounced, pattern emerged for the banks. Their employment as a share of total employment expanded every period from 1960 to 1980 except for the initial period from 1960 to 1965. More recently, the share of the banks has fluctuated without any clear trend from 1976 through 1982. Nevertheless, the growth in employment in the banks has been substantially greater than the industrial sector at large. Over the period as a whole, the banks increased their share of industrial employment by 40 percent, from 2.3 percent of industrial employment in 1960 to 3.2 percent in 1982.

EARNINGS IN THE DEPOSIT-TAKING SECTOR

Availability of Data

Data on average weekly earnings, like the data on employment, are not available continuously for a definition that corresponds to the deposit-taking sector. Table 17 presents the available series that can be used to represent the weekly earnings paid in the deposit-taking sector. The longest running series, that for financial institutions, includes investment companies and security dealers and other credit agencies in addition to deposit-taking institutions. From 1979 onward, a narrower aggregate, savings and credit institutions, has been presented that includes only other credit agencies in addition to deposit-taking institutions.

Table 17

Average Weekly Earnings in the Deposit-Taking Sector

(dollars per week)

Year (mid)	702-704 Financial Institutions	702 Savings and Credit	850-899 Service	630-699 Retail Trade	031-899 Industrial Composite
1960	65.17		52.49	57.34	75.67
1965	85.09		64.39	66.66	90.98
1970	115.92		89.89	86.53	126.12
1975	187.62		143.04	141.76	202.80
1976	210.82		159.90	152.18	225.51
1977	225.41		170.43	164.24	248.31
1978	238.91	231.12	178.43	174.64	264.21
1979	261.38	250.10	194.71	190.20	289.72
1980	290.03	276.39	209.53	200.34	312.46
1981	351.38	333.77	231.68	218.59	352.41
1982	393.85	387.03	258.60	236.14	387.25
1983	417.77	395.33	334.0*	237.12	388.22
1984	431.43	416.23	354.34	250.18	404.56
1985	438.22	415.77	360.49	257.33	419.47

Source: Statistics Canada, Employment and Earnings, 72-002.

Note: * Category now 801-899.

While the narrower aggregates should represent the movements of weekly earnings for employees in the deposit-taking sector most closely, even the broader aggregates will reflect these movements because of the predominance of the deposit-taking sector. As an illustration, consider the composition of each of the measures as of June 1985. At that time, employment in the deposit-taking sector was 242,000. Addition of other credit agencies to give the category of savings and credit institutions only yields another 17,400 employees. Similarly, inclusion of the employees of investment companies and security dealers to give the category financial institutions only adds another 44,300 employees. Thus, deposit-taking institutions account for 93 percent of the employees in the category of savings and credit institutions and even 80 percent of the employees in the larger category of financial institutions.

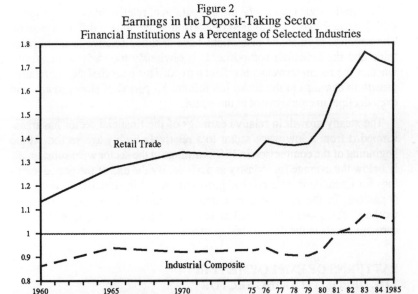

Figure 2
Earnings in the Deposit-Taking Sector
Financial Institutions As a Percentage of Selected Industries

Note: Interpolation between 1960-65, 1965-70, and 1970-75.

Data are also presented in table 17 for a number of other sectors as a basis of comparison. The industrial composite is the broadest measure and best represents the prevailing level of weekly earnings for the rest of the economy. The service sector as a whole has been included to determine the movement of earnings in the deposit-taking sector relative to the rest of the service sector. Unfortunately, the series for the service sector is not consistent for the whole period, having a break in 1983. As a result, data for the retail trade sector are presented to provide a comparison with another major service sector. Figure 2 shows earnings in the deposit-taking sector expressed as a proportion of the earnings in the other sectors.

Trends in Earnings in the Deposit-Taking Sector

Figure 2 shows that the earnings for the financial sector, the aggregate closest to the deposit-taking sector, were only 86 percent of the industrial sector in 1960. On the other hand, earnings of employees in financial institutions exceeded those in retail trade by 13 percent. Throughout the period from 1960 to 1983, earnings in financial institutions increased consistently relative to all the other sectors, increasing 54 percent relative to retail trade, and 25 percent relative to the industrial composite.

Only at the end of the period did this pattern of relative increase reverse itself. The final two years of the comparison show quite a different pattern. The earnings at financial institutions have declined relative to all of retail trade and the industrial composite. It is obviously too early to determine whether the recent movements reflect a trend. This period of slower relative growth in earnings in the sector has followed a period of slow growth, and even decline, in employment in the sector.

The steady growth in relative earnings of the financial sector has transformed it from a low wage sector to a relatively high wage sector. At the beginning of the comparison in 1960, earnings in the sector were substantially below the average for industry as a whole. By the end of the period, earnings for financial institutions had grown to exceed the industrial average by 4 percent. In the next section, attention is turned to an examination of workers' skills and educational attainment as one of the causes of higher earnings levels in the deposit-taking sector.

PATTERNS OF EMPLOYMENT IN THE DEPOSIT-TAKING SECTOR

Many observers have been concerned about the effects of the growth of service industries on the quality of employment in the economy. They fear that service industries will provide either low wage jobs for the bulk of workers in traditional service industries or high incomes for only relatively few workers in areas using advanced technology. The deposit-taking industry provides a good opportunity for examining the validity of this concern, especially because of its substantial size in terms of total service sector employment and its rapid growth in employment.

Skills of Employees

Information has been collected decennially through the Census of Population on the levels of educational attainment achieved by employees in different industries by region. Data on the skills of workers in the deposit-taking sector do not offer any support for the bimodality hypothesis. This sector employs a labour force that has high skills relative to the rest of the economy. At the same time, employment in the sector is spread across a range of skills and is not concentrated in the very highest skill category. The comparisons between the deposit-taking sector (SIC 701) and industry as a whole, presented in figure 3, show that the deposit-taking sector employed a smaller proportion than industry as whole of the two least skilled groups (less than grade 9 and grades 9 to 13 without a certificate) by a margin of 20 percent for SIC 701 to 37 percent for industry; deposit-taking institutions employed a

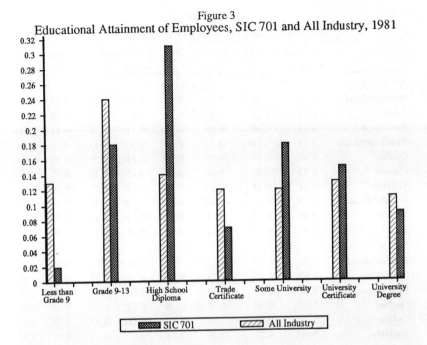

Figure 3
Educational Attainment of Employees, SIC 701 and All Industry, 1981

larger proportion of the three most skilled groups (some university, university with a certificate or diploma, and university degree) by 44 percent for the deposit-taking sector to 34 percent for industry; and the deposit-taking sector employed a slightly smaller proportion of the highest sector (university degree) than industry as a whole.

These comparisons on a national level can be criticized on the grounds that the apparently high skill characteristics could reflect a concentration of employment in areas of the country with relatively high skill levels and that region by region the industry offers employment in the lower skill categories. Table 18 on the skill characteristics by regions offers evidence against this conjecture. The national experience is shown without exception to be repeated for every province: workers in the deposit-taking industry have relatively high skills compared to workers in the rest of industry.

The data derived from the 1981 Census indicate the types of workers employed in the deposit-taking sector at any time, but do not indicate how the pattern of skills has changed over time. The change has particular importance because it indicates the types of skills required for the new jobs created in this industry.

Table 18

Educational Attainment of Employees by Province, 1981

	Less than Grade 9	Gr.9-13 No cert.	Gr.9-13 Cert.	Trade Cert.	Some Univ No cert.	Univ. Cert.	Univ. Degree	Total
All Industry								
Newfoundland	0.23	0.24	0.11	0.17	0.10	0.08	0.07	1.01
P.E.I.	0.18	0.27	0.09	0.14	0.12	0.12	0.08	1.01
Nova Scotia	0.14	0.28	0.09	0.17	0.11	0.11	0.11	1.00
New Brunswick	0.19	0.24	0.13	0.13	0.10	0.11	0.10	1.01
Quebec	0.18	0.16	0.18	0.13	0.11	0.15	0.10	1.00
Ontario	0.12	0.26	0.14	0.11	0.12	0.13	0.12	1.00
Manitoba	0.14	0.31	0.10	0.10	0.12	0.12	0.10	1.00
Saskatchewan	0.15	0.32	0.10	0.11	0.12	0.12	0.08	1.00
Alberta	0.08	0.29	0.12	0.13	0.14	0.13	0.12	1.00
B.C.	0.08	0.27	0.13	0.13	0.15	0.13	0.10	1.00
SIC 701								
Newfoundland	0.00	0.17	0.17	0.31	0.20	0.11	0.04	1.00
Nova Scotia	0.00	0.25	0.25	0.17	0.18	0.11	0.04	1.00
New Brunswick	0.02	0.20	0.30	0.07	0.16	0.18	0.08	1.00
Quebec	0.03	0.10	0.36	0.09	0.17	0.19	0.07	1.00
Ontario	0.01	0.19	0.30	0.05	0.18	0.15	0.11	1.00
Manitoba	0.01	0.30	0.28	0.05	0.17	0.14	0.07	1.00
Saskatchewan	0.02	0.30	0.25	0.06	0.21	0.05	0.13	1.02
Alberta	0.01	0.25	0.28	0.06	0.20	0.12	0.08	1.00
B.C.	0.01	0.21	0.31	0.05	0.22	0.13	0.07	1.00

Source: Census 1981.

Note: No data available for P.E.I. for SIC 701 category.

Table 19

Comparison of Educational Attainment of Employees

All Industry and Deposit-Taking Sector, 1971 and 1981

	Less than Grade 9	Grade 9&10	Grade 11	Grade 12&13	Some Univ.	Univ. Degree	Total
Canada							
1971	0.27	0.23	0.12	0.23	0.08	0.07	1.00
	0.27		0.58		0.08	0.07	
1981	0.13		0.50		0.25	0.11	
SIC 701							
1971	0.04	0.13	0.20	0.49	0.10	0.04	1.00
	0.04		0.82		0.10	0.04	
1981	0.02		0.56		0.33	0.09	

Source: Census for 1971 and 1981.

Table 19 presents a comparison of the skills of employees for the deposit-taking sector and industry as a whole between 1971 and 1981. The difference in categories between 1971 and 1981 restrict the comparison to only four classes. In addition, the overall level of skills increased substantially for industrial employees over the decade.

Despite these complications, a clear pattern of change can be identified. While as at present, the deposit-taking sector employed a smaller proportion of workers from the least skilled group than the rest of industry, it accounted for the same proportion of the two lowest skill categories as industry as a whole in 1971. By 1981, this pattern had changed substantially; only 58 percent of workers in the deposit-taking sector came from the two lowest skill categories compared to 63 percent in industry as a whole. This change in the relative patterns of employment suggests that not only does the deposit-taking sector hire employees with above average skills but it has increasingly directed its hiring toward more skilled workers relative to the rest of industry.

Occupational Distribution

Another perspective on the bimodality hypothesis can be gained from examining the occupation structure in the deposit-taking sector. The Ontario Task Force on Employment and New Technology present data showing the occupation distribution of employees at deposit-taking institutions in Ontario at both the two-digit and four-digit level for 1981 as in table 20. In addition, the rates of growth are shown for each occupation over the period 1971-81. These data offer support for the view that the employment opportunities in the deposit-taking sector have not been concentrated in only the lowest skilled occupations.

Over the period, employment grew by 6.4 percent per year. At the two-digit occupational level, two occupations grew more slowly than the industry average and two grew more rapidly. The primary group that grew more slowly consisted of clerical related positions, a relatively low skilled occupation. In contrast, natural sciences, engineering and mathematics grew most rapidly at 13.1 percent per annum, or 6.7 percent above the growth of employment overall. The other rapidly growing occupation group was managerial, administrative and related which grew at 9 percent per annum.

The four-digit occupational grouping provides little more information than is available at the two-digit level because only the clerical and related group has enough subcategories to make any analysis possible. Electronic data-processing clerks, supervisors (bookkeeping, accounting, and related), and insurance, bank and other finance clerks are the fastest growing

Table 20

Occupational Indicators for Deposit-Taking Institutions, 1971-1981

	Number of employees	Annual average rate of change (percent)
	1981	1971-81
Total Industry	94,835	6.4
Two-Digit Level		
Sales	1,150	(0.6)
Clerical and related	65,375	6.0
Managerial, administrative and related	22,930	9.0
Natural sciences, engineering and mathematics	2,555	13.1
Four-Digit Level		
Clerical and related		
Supervisors, other clerical and related, n.e.s.	650	(4.5)
General office clerks	1,370	1.3
Typists and clerk typists	3,015	1.6
Bookkeepers and accounting clerks	9,410	4.3
Other clerical and related n.e.s.	1,500	5.1
Secretaries and stenographers	5,005	5.1
Tellers and cashiers	22,350	6.6
Insurance, bank and other finance clerks	11,515	9.1
Supervisors, bookkeeping, account recording and related	3,650	11.9
Electronic data processing equipment operators	2,620	13.6
Other	4,290	—
Managerial, administrative and related		
Accountants, auditors and other financial officers	8,495	1.2
Financial management	11,120	28.6
Other	3,315	—
Natural sciences, engineering and mathematics		
Systems analysts, computer programmers and related	2,065	14.8
Other	490	—

Source: *Ontario Task Force on Employment and New Technology.*

Table 21

Full-Time Employees, by Organization/Salary Level,

for Canadian Chartered Banks, 1975 and 1984

Organization Level	Salary Level*	1975 Number	Percent	1984 Number	Percent
Senior Management	$57,000+	1,734	1.42	2,021	1.48
Middle Management	$31,000–57,000	11,439	9.34	20,542	15.08
Junior Management/Supervisory	$19,000–31,000	40,922	33.40	43,426	1.87
Administrative Support	$19,000	68,439	55.85	70,260	51.57
Total		122,534		136,249	

Source: The Canadian Bankers' Association.

Note: * Expressed in 1984 terms.

categories in this group. The growth in two of these categories appears to reflect a changing classification of similar positions in that the more rapid growth in finance appears to offset the slower growth of general office clerks, typists and clerk typists, and bookkeepers and accounting clerks. Therefore, although a considerable shift in occupational distribution of employees may appear to have occurred from examination of the data, much of this shift can be attributed to a reclassification of similar tasks that reflect an adaptation to the introduction of new technology.

Organization and Salary Level

A final set of data for testing the bimodality hypothesis consists of a classification of employees of the chartered banks by organization level for the years 1975 and 1984, shown in table 21. Employees are divided into four groups according to salary level expressed in 1984 terms: senior management, middle management, junior management/supervisory, and administrative support. As can be seen, the bulk of employees in both years were in the lowest category, with the second most in junior management/supervisory. In each of the years, these two categories accounted for over 80 percent of the employment in banking, though their relative importance has declined. These two categories have decreased in significance from 1975 to 1984, with administrative support falling from 55.8 percent to 51.6 percent and junior management from 33.4 percent to 31.9 percent. The category middle management gained the whole of the losses of the two lower groups, increasing its share of total employment from 9.7 percent to 15.1 percent, an increase of over 55 percent.

The Bimodality Hypothesis: Conclusions

The bimodality hypothesis suggests that the employment opportunities created by the growth of service industries tend to be either concentrated in low level, unskilled jobs for many or highly skilled positions for a few. The evidence from the deposit-taking sector provides substantial evidence against this view on the basis of data with respect to skills, occupation, and organization level and salary.

All the evidence reviewed suggests that the pattern of employment in the deposit-taking sector has not been concentrated in lower level positions. Evidence presented in the previous section has shown that earnings in the deposit-taking sector have grown from lower levels so as to become equal to those of industry as a whole, even while employment in this service sector was expanding relative to the rest of industry. The evidence of this section showed that the employees of the deposit-taking sector are better educated than industrial employees overall. Finally, evidence on occupation and organization level show that employment in the deposit-taking sector has shifted toward higher rated positions.

REGIONAL DIMENSIONS OF EMPLOYMENT

The pattern of employment in the deposit-taking sector has been determined in the past, in large part, by two separate forces: the need to provide face-to-face service to many customers, and the centralization of some corporate activities at head offices or regional centres. Personnel were required at local branches in order to carry out deposit and loan transactions with customers and to maintain the records associated with customers' accounts. The head office functions included, in addition to the usual administrative functions of other corporations, the trading in securities' markets in response to deficiencies or surpluses of liquid funds.

The resulting distribution of employment in the deposit-taking sector, shown in table 7 in chapter 2, reflected these influences. Employment in this sector is spread throughout the country, reflecting the geographical distribution of branches fairly closely. The main departure from this pattern is Ontario, where 38.9 percent of bank employees are located compared with only 35.7 percent of the population. This difference appears to be a consequence of the concentration of head offices in that province.

Technological developments in the industry have reduced the constraints locating employment at the local branches. Many transactions arising from deposits now require neither contact with customers nor ready access to paper-based accounting records. Instead, these transactions can be activated

Table 22

Percentage Growth in Employment: Deposit-Taking Sector

	Percentage Change in Employment
Newfoundland	−12.80
Prince Edward Island	−9.10
Nova Scotia	−6.60
New Brunswick	−9.60
Quebec	−7.30
Ontario	10.40
Manitoba	−5.90
Saskatchewan	9.00
Alberta	15.30
British Columbia	2.40
Canada	3.00

Source: DRIE, Employment Dynamics.

service industries over the period from 1978 to 1984. The data for the deposit-taking industry, presented in table 22 show quite substantial changes in the distribution of employment. Employment has declined absolutely in the Maritimes and in Quebec. In addition, major shifts in employment have occurred toward Alberta, Ontario and Manitoba. While the reasons for the particular pattern of shifts remain unclear, they are unlikely to be explained by changing demands for financial services among regions. Shifts of this magnitude would appear possible only as a result of the introduction of technology that offers more flexibility in the location of employment.

UNIONS IN THE DEPOSIT-TAKING SECTOR

The degree of unionization in the deposit-taking sector has continually remained a much smaller proportion of the employees than in the rest of the economy. Tables 23 and 24 present data that show a consistent pattern of low membership for all of Canada and for Ontario. The Canadian data, based on returns under the Corporations and Labour Unions Returns Act, indicate that only 7,000 of the 239,900 workers in the deposit-taking sector during 1984 were unionized (slightly less than 3 percent). Even more extreme are the Ontario data derived from collective bargaining data that suggest that only 0.6 percent of the workers in the industry in Ontario at the time of the survey were unionized.

Table 23

Unionization in the Deposit-Taking Sector in Canada, 1984

Canadian Labour Congress	516
United Steel Workers	205
United Food & Comm. Workers	706
Office & Prof. Employees	3,540
C.S.D.	371
United Auto Workers	73
International Woodworkers	17
Fed. du Commerce	1,372
Fed. des Prof. Salaries et des Cadres du P.Q.	3
C.U.P.E.	176
R.W.D.S.U. Sask (joint board)	39
Total	7,018

Source: Filings under the Corporations and Labour Unions Returns Act.

Table 24

Unionization in the Deposit-Taking Sector for Ontario, 1984

Name of Union	Employer	Members
Office and Professional Employees	Soo & District of Algoma C.U.	56
	Hamilton-Wentworth Credit Union	50
	Auto Workers Oshawa Credit Union	44
	West Fort William Credit Union	38
	Stelco Employees Primary Works C.U.	37
	Cuna of Ontario Credit Union	16
	Northland Savings & Credit Union	12
	Twin Oak Industrial Credit Union	11
United Auto Workers	Family Savings and Credit Union Niagara	45
	Motorco & Windsor	18
United Steelworkers	ASCU Community Credit Union	36
Canadian Brewery Workers	Canada Trustco Mortgage	19
Canadian Labour Congress	Brant Community Credit Union	14
	Bank of Nova Scotia	10
Food & Commercial Workers	Bank of Montreal	14
Independent	Airline Malton Credit Union	12

Source: *Ontario Task Force on Employment and New Technology,* Employment and New Technology in the Chartered Banks and Trust Industry: An Appendix to the Final Report, p. 52.

The Ontario data give a clear indication of the areas of the industry that have been unionized. Although credit unions account for only a small proportion of the employees in the sector, they employed 487 of the union members in the province, while trust companies employed 19 and the chartered banks only 24. Since the time of the survey, a major change has occurred with the certification by the Union of Bank Employees of 200 employees at the Bank of Commerce's Visa centre in Toronto during October 1984 (Ontario Task Force 1985).

The data presented for Ontario and Canada do not appear to be entirely consistent. While both sets of data show relatively low rates of unionization, the rate of 3 percent indicated for Canada is over five times the 0.6 percent rate found in Ontario. The relatively high rate of unionization for credit union employees found in Ontario may help to reconcile the differences. The share of credit unions in the deposit-taking sector is much higher than in Ontario in other regions of the country, most notably Quebec, Saskatchewan and British Columbia. The same or a higher incidence of unionization among credit union employees in these provinces would lead to higher unionization rates for the deposit-taking sector as a whole relative to those found in Ontario.

The low level of unionization found in the deposit-taking industry has been attributed by some to the organization of business activity into branch offices.[2] Historically, labour boards have used the employer's business structure in defining the relevant bargaining unit. In the case of the banks, the bargaining unit typically consisted of all the branches in a region. Dunsmore argues that "the longstanding requirement for a larger unit had frustrated organizing attempts in the bank sector because unions alleged it was difficult to sign up the majority of employees in a region" (1986).

The Canada Labor Relations Board revised its policy and ruled in 1977 that single branches could be regarded as bargaining units. Despite the expectations held for this step at the time, some writers argue that the organization of single branches does not give the unions the strength to bargain effectively. Indeed, subsequent to this decision, some chartered banks excluded organized branches from their overall wage and salary increases (Lowe 1980).

A number of recent decisions of labour boards may alter the strength of unions in the deposit-taking sector. In three separate instances, different labour boards have permitted unions to organize groups of selected branches in a region that do not correspond to the employer's administrative divisions. Dunsmore states that "the prospect of multi-branch units means unions will bargain with greater strength than would be the case with individual units" (1986). This change in practice by labour boards does appear to affect the costs of organizing employees in the deposit-taking sector. Whether the rate of unionization increases in response remains to be seen.

EMPLOYEE PRODUCTIVITY IN THE DEPOSIT-TAKING SECTOR

Measurement of Employee Productivity

The assessment of the changes in employee productivity in the deposit-taking sector is complicated by two conceptual problems. The first problem, which is unique to the deposit-taking sector, arises because of difficulties in making comparisons of the output of the deposit-taking sector on a year-to-year basis (mentioned in chapter 3).

The other problem arises because product per employee as an indicator of productivity fails to include the labour used by customers in gaining the benefits of the industry's services. As discussed in chapter 2, many of the services of intermediaries, especially payments services, require the use of customers' time and effort.

Table 25

Output per Employee in Deposit-Taking Institutions, 1978 to 1985

Real Output	1978	1979	1980	1981	1982	1983	1984	1985
Gross domestic product	2308.4	2432.9	2439.8	2585.8	2535.3	2399.9	2354.1	2464.3
Employment in savings and credit institutions	203400	214600	216500	217700	221500	237600	239900	259400
GDP per employee	11349.1	11336.9	11269.3	11877.8	11446.0	10100.6	9812.8	9500.0

Source: Tables 14 and 16.

Employee Productivity Over Time

Productivity in the deposit-taking sector can be measured by the indexes of domestic product per employee presented in table 25 for the years 1978 to 1985, the only years for which these data are available on a consistent basis.[3] In the early years of the period, from 1978 to 1982, gross domestic product per employee grew by less than 1 percent, increasing in only one year, 1980 to 1981. This period of slow growth was followed in 1983 and 1984 by a substantial decrease in product per worker of almost 6 percent. Overall, gross domestic product per employee appears to have decreased slightly in the period under review.

The absence of any increase of output per employee contrasts with the experience from 1961 to 1975 studied by Geehan and Allen (1978). They found a reformulation of the product accounts for savings and credit institutions indicated that output per employee increased by 2.3 percent per year. Closer examination of the Geehan and Allen study suggests that the differences between the two periods may not be as pronounced as first appearances suggest. Geehan and Allen found that the output growth was not steady, decreasing in the recession years of 1970 and 1975. In addition, their study indicates that most of the growth in output per employee occurred prior to 1972, and that from 1972 to 1975 output per worker was essentially stable. The finding of the current study that output per employee did not increase between 1978 and 1983 appears to be consistent with the pattern of the later years studied by Geehan and Allen.

The lack of change in output per employee in the deposit-taking sector does not appear to correspond to the image of this sector as one which has been experiencing rapid innovation. It lends support to those who argue that productivity change will be limited in service industries because of their intensive use of labour. The finding that output per employee did not increase between 1978 and 1984 does not mean productivity failed to increase over the period. As has been discussed earlier in chapter 2, labour is used in two separate ways in the deposit-taking sector. Labour is employed directly as a productive input in producing financial services. In addition to this labour directly employed in the sector, labour must also be applied by users of the industry's output to gain the full benefits of its services. Thus, increases in productivity can reduce either of the labour inputs. When an innovation occurs in the internal processes of the deposit-taking industry, it results in an increase in output per worker. On the other hand, when the innovation occurs in the nature of services offered by the industry, it represents an improvement in the quality of output and escapes measurement even though it may result in saving of effort by the customers of financial institutions.

The difference between the two types of innovation and their effects on quality change can be illustrated by an example. Suppose that prior to innovation, a deposit transaction took two minutes of teller time and ten minutes of customer time, including travel and standing in line in addition to the actual time spent carrying out the transaction. The introduction of an automated teller might increase the time spent by bank employees to three minutes per transaction but reduce the time spent by customers to five minutes per transaction. If the effect of this innovation is measured purely in terms of bank employees, productivity would appear to have fallen from two minutes per transaction before to three minutes per transaction afterwards. In terms of overall labour requirements, this innovation represents an improvement in productivity in that the total time requirements for the transaction have decreased from twelve minutes (two minutes for tellers and ten for customers) to eight minutes (three for tellers and five for customers) per transaction. Conventional measures of productivity such as those used above fail to capture the improved quality of the product in terms of reducing the customer's time and effort.

The pattern of innovations over the period is consistent with the movements that occurred in output per employees. The early part of the period that was studied by Geehan and Allen coincided with a period in which the majority of the innovations were applications of computers to the internal procedures of the banks. At the beginning of that period, the banks introduced MICR (magnetic ink character recognition) encoding and batch processing that streamlined cheque processing. These innovations were followed in 1965 by online systems that enabled record keeping to be removed from the branch. Each of these innovations would be expected to decrease the labour requirements for supplying banking services.

The pattern of innovations has changed in more recent years. Bank cards and cash dispensers represent the first in a wave of innovations that reduce customer time and effort. Even more significant for the consumer has been the introduction of automated banking machines in 1970 and multi-branch banking and daily interest accounts in 1975. For the business customer, the introduction of direct deposit/tape exchange in 1975 and pre-authorized payments in 1982 all tended to reduce the customer's labour requirements for gaining the benefits of the services of this industry.

Summary: Employee Productivity

In summary, the measured changes in output per employee suggest that productivity did not increase in the deposit-taking sector over the period from 1972 to 1983. This result does not rule out the possibility of productivity increase, counting both internal and external use of labour. In the years 1961 to 1972 when innovation occurred mainly in internal procedures, substantial increases occurred in output per worker. In the subsequent period, the major innovations changed the nature of the services offered to customers and would not be expected to have a major impact on output per employee. The degree to which these innovations decreased the labour requirements of the customers of deposit-taking institutions remains an open question.

NOTES

1. The series on employment presented in table 15 differ in one important respect that makes strict comparisons impossible. The data from Statistics Canada include all employees, including part-time employees, whereas the data from the Canadian Bankers' Association and from the Trust Companies' Association both exclude part-time employees. This difference in coverage appears to account for some of the differential movements in the series, especially in the 1980s.

2. See Ross Dunsmore, *Financial Times*, November 17, 1986.

3. Note that a lack of consistency in the employment data means that comparisons of per employee measures cannot be made between the period up to 1982 and the period after.

Chapter 5

TAXATION OF DEPOSIT-TAKING INSTITUTIONS

The taxation of deposit-taking institutions raises a number of complicated issues. Some are shared with other corporations that receive investment income, some are general to financial institutions as a whole, and some are unique to particular financial institutions. The general issue of the taxation of investment income will be considered first. It is to be followed by a discussion of the problems in taxing particular financial institutions.

TAXATION OF INVESTMENT INCOME

The taxation of investment income differs according to the form of income, interest or dividends, and the recipient of the income, private or public corporation. Complications arise because of the desire to avoid "double taxation"—taxation of the income in the hands of both the corporation earning the income initially and the corporation receiving the interest and dividends. The following discussion will concentrate on the treatment of public corporations because the major deposit-taking institutions take this form.

The dividend income received by Canadian public corporations is treated so as to avoid double taxation by excluding any dividends received by public corporations from its taxable income. As the major deposit-taking institutions are public corporations, this treatment is accorded to their dividend income.

The treatment of interest income received by corporations differs between private and public corporations. Double taxation is avoided in the case of private corporations by the effective integration of the corporation's tax with that of its owner. The owner gains a credit for the taxes paid by the corporation through a combination of tax refunds for the corporation and the dividend tax credit for the owner. The effect of these provisions makes any investment income flowing through private corporations free from the corporate income tax.

This treatment is not accorded to the interest income received by public corporations. Deposit-taking institutions and other public corporations must include interest receipts in their taxable income. They are, however, allowed to deduct the expenses incurred in earning this income, including the expense of interest paid to depositors.

The taxation of interest income received by deposit-taking institutions may appear anomalous relative to the treatment of private corporations. Conceptually, however, it can be justified by reference to the nature of intermediation. As discussed in chapter 3, the income of intermediaries arises from the spread between the interest rates that they receive and the rates that they pay; thus these spreads can be considered to be the fee for intermediation or, alternatively, the sales revenues of intermediaries. Failure to include this revenue as taxable income would mean that intermediaries would have only the revenues generated by explicit service charges.

Financial institutions, in general, thus are treated the same as other public corporations. As Boadway and Kitchen observe, "all the rules applicable to the taxation of corporate income apply to them. They pay the full corporate rate of 46 per cent on taxable income which includes interest earned and one-half of capital gains but excludes intercorporate dividends" (1984:138).

TAXATION OF BANKS

Chartered banks are treated differently for tax purposes than other public corporations and deposit-taking institutions in a number of ways. The chartered banks have special tax treatment of reserves for losses, are subject to provincial capital taxes, and are treated differently in terms of the withholding tax on interest payments to non-residents. In addition, the banks and their borrowers have participated in so-called after tax financing. Finally, the chartered banks are subject to a unique form of implicit taxation: a requirement to hold non-interest bearing cash reserves at the Bank of Canada.

Reserves for Losses

Chartered banks are permitted to deduct additions to reserves to cover losses on loans and bad and doubtful debts from their taxable income in any year. This provision appears justifiable if the additions to reserves correspond to actual losses given the prospect that not all the accrued income from loans in any year will actually be realized. The provisions appear to be a reasonable attempt to approximate the income that will eventually be realized from current accruals.

The appropriation to the reserve in any year is determined by the actual loan loss experience and recoveries in the current year. In addition, the amount that can be deducted in any year is subject to two limitations: the annual allocation to the reserve cannot exceed the five-year moving average of loss experience on loans, and since 1974 the total reserve cannot exceed 1.5 percent of eligible assets less than $1 billion and 1 percent of eligible assets in excess of $1 billion.

Provincial Capital Taxes

Chartered banks are subject to a set of provincial taxes that are specific to banking. The provinces of British Columbia, Saskatchewan, Manitoba, Ontario, Quebec and Newfoundland all levy capital taxes on banks with permanent establishments in their province. In addition, the federal government imposed a 1 percent capital tax through 1986 and 1987 on banks and trust and loan companies where capital exceeds $300 million.[1] Power and Varma report that "a bank's taxable capital includes its paid-up capital, retained earnings and other surpluses, and all booked reserves not deductible for income tax purposes on a non-consolidated basis" (1984:74).

The taxable capital of any bank in a province is determined by a formula that depends "on the combined percentage of salaries, wages, loans and deposits averaged on a monthly basis attributed to each province" (Varma and Power, p. 74). The rates differ among the provinces and range from 0.8 percent to 2 percent of capital, whereas the federal rate was 1 percent. Capital taxes are considered an operating expense for the purposes of determining taxable income for the corporate income tax.

After Tax Funding

The taxation of banks has been affected by their holdings of securities that are tax exempt, namely term-preferred shares, income debentures, and Small Business Development Bonds. Each of the instruments enables banks and other financial institutions to carry out lending transactions in specified ways and avoid a liability for taxes on the resulting income.

Each of these instruments differ in detail. Term-preferred shares pay a dividend that has priority over the dividend on common shares and also entitle the holder to repayment at a fixed value under specified conditions. Income debentures are securities on which interest is paid only if sufficient income is earned by the borrower and is repayable at a fixed date. Finally, Small Business Development Bonds are securities on which interest payments are neither deductible by the borrower nor taxable to the lender.

The use of any of these instruments gives a tax advantage to borrowing and lending when the borrower does not have any taxable income and, as a result, does not gain any advantage from the ability to use interest as an expense for tax purposes. With any of these instruments, an advantage arises because the "interest" or its equivalent is not taxed in the hands of the lender. As a consequence, the borrower benefits to the extent that the interest rate required by the lender is lower than otherwise. The Finance Committee of the House of Commons stated that "the after-tax revenue generated by 'loan substitutes' should be considered a transfer of after-tax revenue from one company to another" (p. 117).

Cash Reserves as a Tax

Chartered banks, alone among deposit-taking institutions, are required to hold cash reserves at the Bank of Canada equal to some minimum proportion of their different deposit liabilities. Beginning in 1980, the minimum cash reserve ratio for each chartered bank has been 10 percent of Canadian dollar demand deposits, 2 percent of Canadian dollar notice deposits plus 1 percent of Canadian dollar notice deposits in excess of $500 million, and 3 percent of foreign currency deposits with branches and offices in Canada.[2]

The minimum cash reserve requirement has been justified as being required for the purposes of monetary policy. It is argued that without reserve requirements the response of banks to monetary policy would be sufficiently unpredictable so as to limit the central bank's control over the money supply. Regardless of its justification, the minimum cash reserve requirement serves as an implicit tax on the chartered banks in that they are required to hold cash reserves that do not yield any interest. Moreover, the cash held to satisfy the reserve requirement can be regarded as an indirect claim on the federal government. In effect, the tax on the banks equals the yield that the banks could have earned if they were free to choose other assets. In as much as banks would likely hold some cash reserves in absence of reserve requirements in order to meet the cash withdrawals that occur in day-to-day business, the cost of the reserve tax would equal the interest forgone on the additional reserves held because of the reserve requirements.

Some perspective on the significance of this implicit tax can be gained from examining the banks' cash reserve holdings during 1985 when the chartered banks were required to maintain a minimum average reserve requirement of 3.89 percent of statutory deposits or, in absolute terms, $5.3 billion on average over the year. With the average Treasury bill rate over the year of 9.54 percent as the measure of the forgone return, the revenue losses to the banks would have been over $250 million if half of the actual reserves were held voluntarily and $375 million if only one-quarter of reserves were held voluntarily.

The additional costs of intermediation resulting from the minimum reserve requirement can be judged by comparing them to the difference between the interest received and the interest paid by banks, the best measure of the costs of intermediation to bank customers. During 1985, this spread measured approximately $10.5 billion on all the business, foreign and domestic, of the chartered banks. If the interest spread were allocated proportionately to the net interest income, $6.6 billion of this amount was earned on domestic business. In this case, the reserve tax accounted for between 3.8 percent and 5.7 percent of the cost of supplying bank services to domestic residents.

These costly reserve requirements that apply only to chartered banks may soon be eliminated entirely. The federal government observes in its *New Directions for the Financial System* that these requirements "have the side effect of imposing unequal costs on institutions competing for the same business" (p. 12) and proposes that they be phased out beginning in 1990.

TAXATION OF CREDIT UNIONS

The taxation of credit unions creates a number of problems from the perspective of the corporate income tax. Technically, credit unions are co-operatives and not corporations. On the other hand, credit unions perform the same functions as competitors, and the membership requirement is regarded as a mere formality to some customers. Until 1972, the former argument—that credit unions were not corporations—governed their tax treatment, leaving them untaxable. The tax reform of that year made credit unions subject to the corporation tax with a number of special provisions that are intended to reflect the nature of the business of credit unions.

First, credit unions are permitted to deduct patronage payments to members in proportion to their borrowing. These payments, even though they are determined on the basis of operating results and could be considered as the equivalent to corporate profits, are treated as a reduction in interest revenues earned on loans to members. The second provision affects the tax treatment of credit union income. *Canada Master Tax Guide* describes this provision in the following way:

> A credit union may deduct from the tax otherwise payable an amount equal to 21% of the lesser of (1) the amount by which the corporation's taxable income for the year exceeds the least of the amounts relative to the small business deduction, or (2) the amount by which 4/3 of the corporation's maximum cumulative reserve at the end of the year exceeds

the aggregate of the corporation's preferred-rate amount at the end of the immediately preceding taxation year, plus the least of the amounts relative to the small business deduction (p. 506).

Boadway and Kitchen (1984) suggest that this provision makes the effective tax rates for credit unions equal to the small business tax rate.

TAXATION OF DEPOSIT-TAKING INSTITUTIONS IN PRACTICE

The tax rates paid by deposit-taking institutions in any year differ from the corporate tax because of the particular provisions that apply to different deposit-taking institutions and also because deposit-taking institutions can take advantage of general provisions that apply to their business. The actual taxes paid by and the effective tax rates that apply to deposit-taking institutions can only be determined by examining data with respect to their net income and taxes paid.

Data with respect to the taxes paid by deposit-taking institutions can be obtained from a variety of different sources. The basic source for industrial taxes is *Corporate Financial Statistics*. This source provides detailed data only for the financial sector as a whole without any separate data for the deposit-taking sector. Some summary data are used for comparisons of the deposit-taking sector with other sectors. More complete data, comparable to that for other industries, are presented in Statistics Canada's *Financial Institutions* for deposit-taking institutions as a whole and for chartered banks, trust and loan companies and credit unions separately. Finally, an entirely different set of income and expense data is presented on an annual basis in the *Bank of Canada*.

Unfortunately, the data for income and taxes from the different sources do not agree. Table 26 presents a comparison of the data for the banking sector derived from *Corporate Financial Statistics, Financial Institutions* and the *Bank of Canada Review* to illustrate the problems of lack of comparability. As can be seen, estimates for bank net profit before taxes vary between $1.1 billion and $2.5 billion, whereas the provisions for taxes range from $75 million to $702 million.

Some of the differences in the data appear readily explainable. For example, some differences could be expected because the data from the Bank of Canada are for the financial year ended in 1984, whereas those from Statistics Canada are for the calendar year of 1984. In addition, the data from *Financial Institutions* differ from those of the Bank of Canada by covering only business booked in Canada. Given these differences in their basis, these two sets of data appear reasonably consistent. The data from the *Corporate*

Table 26

Alternative Measures of Bank Profit, 1984

	Corporate Financial Statistics (calendar year)	Financial Institutions (calendar year)	Bank of Canada (financial year)
Net profit before taxes	1884.5	1077.9	2572.4
Non-recurring income	147.7	225.7	
Provision for taxes		478.8	701.1
current	−116.4		
deferred	191.4		
Net profit after tax	1959.6	824.8	1863.6

Note: Data from Financial Institutions are consolidated and booked in Canada.

Financial Statistics appear to be the only data to be inconsistent with the other sources after due allowances for differences in coverage.

For the purposes of this study, the data from *Financial Institutions* will be used for determining the effective tax rates for the deposit-taking sector. This choice has been made because these data appear reasonably consistent with that found in the financial statements of individual institutions.[3] Unfortunately, these data cannot be used for comparisons of deposit-taking institutions and other sectors.

Taxes in the Deposit-Taking Sector

Table 27 presents the net income, the income taxes paid, and the effective tax rate for deposit-taking institutions over the period 1960 to 1985.[4] Two features of these data are particularly significant. First, the effective rate of tax declined substantially from 1960 to the late '70s and early '80s and, although the decline reversed, the subsequent increase has offset only some of the decline. Secondly, the effective tax rate falls considerably below the statutory tax rate.

The difference between actual and effective rates of tax paid by deposit-taking institutions reflects the factors that have been discussed above. The income received by deposit-taking institutions remains untaxed when it is in the form of dividends, interest from income debentures and Small Business Development Loans or capital gains, or comes from foreign subsidiaries subject to tax in another country.

Data provided by individual institutions indicates the relative importance of each of these factors in reducing the effective tax rates. In 1982, the year of the lowest effective tax rate for banks, the Bank of Montreal reported that

Table 27
Income Taxes Paid by Deposit-Taking Institutions

	Chartered Banks (millions of dollars)			Trust Companies (thousands of dollars)			Loan Companies (thousands of dollars)		
	Income Taxes	Net Income Before Taxes	Effective Tax Rate	Income Taxes	Net Income Before Taxes	Effective Tax Rate	Income Taxes	Net Income Before Taxes	Effective Tax Rate
1960	91	197	0.462						
1965	92	258	0.355	15783	34368	0.459	12596	36424	0.346
1970	278	528	0.526	21611	56236	0.384	16664	58091	0.287
1975	591	1234	0.479	50669	125373	0.404	41343	119791	0.345
1976	536	1200	0.447	58456	158478	0.369	38164	107588	0.355
1977	513	1246	0.412	68326	192385	0.355	43038	115998	0.371
1978	518	1495	0.347	72630	218789	0.332	36143	113583	0.318
1979	224	1332	0.168	27218	153390	0.177	14878	92731	0.160
1980	210	1457	0.144	24153	161736	0.149	11624	107320	0.108
1981	455	2175	0.209	-20879	114391	-0.183	9151	107242	0.085
1982	105	1630	0.064	6359	164282	0.039	6367	127329	0.050
1983	813	2723	0.299	88759	326083	0.272	58632	270722	0.217
1984	630	2423	0.260	10450	197704	0.053	-2905	169330	0.017
1985	861	2970	0.290	44413	273374	0.162	90237	338680	0.266

Sources: For chartered banks, *Bank of Canada Review*; and for trust and loan companies, Statistics Canada, Financial Institutions.

dividend income lowered the effective tax rate by 27.4 percentage points, interest on income debentures and Small Business Bonds by 20.3 points, and income from foreign subsidiaries by 17.3 points. Similarly, dividends and exempt interest reduced the effective tax rate for the Canadian Bank of Commerce and the Royal Bank each by roughly the same 27 percentage points.

The recovery of the effective tax rates paid by deposit-taking institutions after 1982 resulted from a number of changes in the treatment of after-tax financing. The federal government took a number of steps in its budget of November 1978 and again in 1982 to prevent banks from avoiding tax through these loan substitutes. The effectiveness of these measures can be illustrated by the difference in the role of dividends in reducing the effective tax paid by the banks. In 1985, a sample of large banks reduced their effective tax rates by only 9 to 15 percentage points as a result of dividends and exempt interest. Nevertheless, it is reported that the six largest banks still held loan substitutes amounting to $6.6 billion in 1987 and that it will take until 1996 for these holdings to shrink to $280 million (*Globe and Mail,* June 16, 1987, B2). Not all this reduction in effective tax rates resulted from the reduction in holding loan substitutes; some resulted from income gained from the banks' subsidiaries that had already been taxed in the subsidiaries' hands.

Comparisons with Other Sectors

Table 28 compares the effective tax rates of the financial sector with those of other major economic sectors. The wide differences in effective tax rates are the result of such factors as the preferential tax rate for small business and deferred taxes from depletion allowances and accelerated depreciation. The lower small business rate serves to explain low effective rates in agriculture, forestry and fisheries, construction, and retail trade. Deferred taxes are likely to be more important in manufacturing, utilities and mining.

This comparison suggests that effective tax rates are generally only a fraction of statutory rates, with the lowest effective rates found in agriculture, mining and financial institutions, insurance and real estate. The average rate for the financial services sector is the lowest of all the major sectors, falling below the average for all industry by 4.2 percentage points.

POLICY ISSUES IN TAXATION

The taxation of financial institutions, especially the chartered banks, remains a controversial issue. To some, the low effective tax rates show that financial institutions are the epitome of "corporate welfare bums." The low effective

Table 28

Average Federal Tax Rates As a Percentage of Financial Statement Income

Sector	Average Tax Rate
Agriculture, forestry and fishing	16.9
Mining	15
Oil and gas	21.4
Manufacturing	18.9
Construction	20.1
Wholesale trade	24.5
Retail trade	21.2
Financial institutions, insurance and real estate	14.5
Services	20.4
All Industries Total	18.7

Source: Minister of Finance, Tax Reform 1987, Income Tax Reform, p. 43.

Note: The Department of Finance states that "the data are based on various years chosen to be representative of profit and investment performance."

tax rates paid by the deposit-taking institutions may arise from any of several sources. First, they may reflect tax measures designed to make taxation consistent for different types of corporate organizations. Such measures include the exemption from tax of dividends when passing from one taxable corporation to another and the tax treatment of income from foreign subsidiaries that are subject to tax in another country. Secondly, the low tax rates may be caused by measures taken by the government to encourage lending for specific types of activity. The Small Business Development Bond with its tax-exempt interest payments was designed to encourage banks to lend to firms that are starting up and do not currently earn taxable income. Finally, low effective tax rates may result from banks and other deposit-taking institutions exploiting features of the tax system for purposes other than those for which the features were intended.

Preliminary examination of the taxes paid by deposit-taking institutions suggests that these low rates were the consequence of a combination of all three factors. Deposit-taking institutions, banks in particular, receive dividends from subsidiaries in Canada and abroad on which corporate income taxes have already been paid. They have also been active lenders through Small Business Development Loans. Finally, the reactions of the authorities in changing the guidelines for term-preferred shares and income debentures suggests that deposit-taking institutions had been using these instruments to lower their taxes in ways that had not been foreseen by the tax authorities.

The appropriate response to the low effective tax rates paid by the banks differs according to source. In the first two cases, little action is necessary. The legitimate avoidance of double taxation is necessary to prevent the tax system from unduly penalizing certain types of corporate forms, especially when these forms may be required by regulatory concerns. Tax incentives should be monitored to determine that the benefits are sufficient to justify the costs. If they are, no further action is required until the objectives or the costs or benefits change. Action is required when the low tax results from use of tax provisions in unanticipated ways. The closing of loopholes should proceed in ways that do not impair the legitimate objectives of the tax measures.

This study, while suggesting that the presence of all three factors contributed to the low effective tax rates of deposit-taking institutions, has been unable to identify the contribution of each source. Any efforts to raise the seemingly low effective tax rates paid by deposit-taking institutions or otherwise change their tax treatment should be based on a thorough knowledge of the sources of the present levels of taxation. To some extent, concerns with the present system of taxation may be reduced by measures introduced in the anticipated tax reform.[5] Even here, a better understanding of the taxation of financial institutions will be required. The U.S. Treasury reports that "the practical problems of taxing financial services have led all the European Economic Community (ECC) countries to exempt the basic lending activities of banking, insurance, and related financial establishments from the value-added tax" (p. 49).

NOTES

1. See Clarkson Gordon (1987:12).

2. The calculation of the minimum reserve levels to be held in any month is intricate, involving deposit levels and currency holdings in the preceding month. The details of the calculations can be found in Shearer, Chant and Bond (1984).

3. These are also the data used by Mintz (1978) in his important study of the taxation of financial institutions.

4. These data include neither the provincial capital taxes nor the tax equivalent of the required cash reserve ratio.

5. For a critique of the proposals as applied to financial institutions, see J. Chant, "Financial Institutions and Tax Reform" (forthcoming).

Chapter 6

PROFITS AND COSTS OF
DEPOSIT-TAKING SECTOR

This chapter reviews the profits and the costs of the deposit-taking sector. The examination of profits compares the rate of profit in the deposit-taking industry and its variability with those of other industries as a bench-mark. Costs are examined in order to determine the similarities and differences in the use of different inputs in the deposit-taking sector relative to other industries.

PROFITS OF THE DEPOSIT-TAKING SECTOR

The profits of deposit-taking institutions, the chartered banks in particular, have been a subject of much controversy in Canada. In a thorough study of bank profits, Jack Mintz observed "the after-tax profit rate earned by the Canadian bank shareholders increased substantially to an average of 12.8 per cent for the 1968-73 period. Canadian chartered banks also earned an average after-tax rate of return to capital that was 2.2 percentage points greater than the average profit rate earned by all market-oriented sectors after 1963...After the 1967 Bank Act became effective, the before-tax rates of return for the chartered banks were, in all years, higher than those earned by all other sectors" (1978:45-46). Subsequently, bank profits became sufficiently sensitive that in 1983 a committee of the House of Commons held hearings on the topic and issued majority and minority reports.

In this study, the profit performance of the banks will be examined from two perspectives. Attention will be directed first to the profits of deposit-taking institutions as measured on an accounting basis. Subsequently, this profitability will be examined from the perspective of the market's evaluation of the performance of deposit-taking institutions.

Table 29

Return to Equity Before and After Tax, Selected Industries, 1977 to 1984

	1984	1983	1982	1981	1980	1979	1978	1977	Average	Standard Deviation
Agriculture, Forestry and Fisheries										
Before tax return	13.3	10.3	14.0	17.2	30.3	32.5	28.5	18.2	20.5	0.080
After tax return	9.6	7.1	11.1	12.3	23.2	24.3	22.3	30.6	17.6	0.080
Mining										
Before tax return	20.1	17.4	14.8	19.9	33.2	34.3	23.5	24.3	23.5	0.066
After tax return	5.9	5.1	4.5	9.8	20.4	21.8	14.8	14.6	12.1	0.064
Manufacturing										
Before tax return	20.0	12.6	7.4	22.6	25.2	27.3	22.1	18.0	19.4	0.062
After tax return	13.6	8.2	4.3	14.2	15.9	17.4	14.2	11.1	12.4	0.040
Construction										
Before tax return	22.1	18.6	19.7	27.8	27.8	26.6	23.5	23.5	23.7	0.033
After tax return	17.0	12.7	12.8	18.2	18.8	17.9	15.3	14.9	15.9	0.022
Utilities										
Before tax return	15.1	15.4	14.4	15.2	17.2	17.3	15.0	12.6	15.3	0.014
After tax return	10.8	11.3	10.3	12.6	12.4	12.4	10.7	8.8	11.2	0.012
Wholesale Trade										
Before tax return	17.3	12.7	10.1	21.8	26.4	28.4	23.9	19.4	20.0	0.060
After tax return	12.2	8.7	6.1	14.0	16.8	18.9	15.6	12.3	13.1	0.040
Retail Trade										
Before tax return	36.3	36.0	31.7	35.9	38.2	40.0	36.1	31.9	35.8	0.026
After tax return	31.1	31.5	28.0	29.4	30.8	32.3	29.9	25.8	29.9	0.020

Trust Companies										
Before tax return	-1.5	10.2	7.9	7.5	10.6	12.8	18.7	16.5	10.3	0.058
After tax return	-0.5	7.6	7.4	2.5	9.6	10.7	12.7	10.3	7.5	0.042
Loan Companies										
Before tax return	8.0	10.3	9.7	14.8	11.4	1.1	10.7	17.6	10.4	0.045
After tax return	6.4	7.9	7.5	12.2	9.5	-0.1	7.7	13.4	8.0	0.038
Banks										
Before tax return	12.7	15.5	9.1	17.1	7.9	9.6	18.2	19.5	13.7	0.042
After tax return	13.2	14.8	13.8	15.0	0.8	9.6	12.2	11.8	11.4	0.043
All Deposit -taking										
Before tax return	10.3	13.9	9.1	14.0	9.0	8.1	16.4	18.6	12.4	0.036
After tax return	10.5	12.7	11.8	14.0	9.3	7.6	11.2	12.0	11.1	0.019
All Finance										
Before tax return	9.3	7.2	7.2	12.6	12.8	13.1	12.6	11.3	10.8	0.023
After tax return	8.3	6.3	6.8	10.7	10.8	11.1	9.9	8.5	9.0	0.017
All Services										
Before tax return	35.4	30.7	27.1	32.1	36.7	35.8	50.6	25.4	34.2	0.073
After tax return	25.9	21.7	19.1	21.3	24.8	24.7	24.8	16.5	22.3	0.031
All Industries										
Before tax return	15.8	12.8	11.1	18.8	22.4	23.3	19.6	17.0	17.6	0.040
After tax return	11.2	8.7	7.6	12.9	15.5	16.3	13.7	11.4	12.2	0.029
All Non-financial										
Before tax return	20.5	16.6	13.4	22.0	26.9	27.9	22.6	19.5	21.2	0.046
After tax return	13.0	10.3	8.1	14.2	17.7	18.7	15.3	12.7	13.7	0.033

Source: Statistics Canada, Corporate Financial Statistics.

Accounting Profits

Recent profit data for the deposit-taking sector, its components and other major sectors of the economy are presented on a year-by-year basis in table 29 for the years 1977 to 1984. The relative profit performance for the deposit-taking sector appears substantially different from the experience for the banks that was documented by Mintz for an earlier period.

In the present study, the profit rates of the deposit-taking institutions as a whole are compared with those of other major sectors in the economy for the years 1977 to 1984. Data are also presented separately for the profits of the individual components of the deposit-taking sector. The data used for these comparisons are from Statistics Canada, *Corporate Financial Statistics*.[1]

Before Tax Profits

Table 29 shows that the profits of the deposit-taking institutions were below those of most other industry over the period. The deposit-taking industry earned an average rate of profit of 12.4 percent before taxes over the years 1977 to 1984, compared to a rate of 34.2 percent for all services, 21.2 percent for non-financial industry, and 17.6 percent for all industry. In only two years did the before tax return of the deposit-taking sector exceed the return of the average of all industries, and never did it exceed that of all services or the non-financial sector as a whole. Over the period, the rate of profit before taxes in the deposit-taking sector ranked last out of eight major sectors of the economy.

Substantial differences in before tax returns existed within the deposit-taking sector. The return of the banks averaged 13.7 percent, well above the average of 10.3 percent for the trust companies, and 10.4 percent for the mortgage loan companies. As a result of past controversy, it is interesting to compare the profits of the chartered banks with those of other industrial sectors. The before tax return of the banks was 13.7 percent compared to the 12.4 percent for deposit-taking institutions as a whole. Even this difference is insufficient to change the relative ranking. Over the decade, the banks would have been in last place among major industries.

After Tax Profits

Table 29 also presents the after tax profits for the deposit-taking sector, its components and other major sectors of the economy. These data would give exactly the same relative ranking for the different industries as the before tax data if all the sectors were subject to the same effective tax rate. The table, however, indicates substantial differences in effective tax rates running from the 49 percent rate indicated for the mining industry to the 10 percent rate for the deposit-taking industry.

The profit performance of the deposit-taking industry is relatively better on an after tax basis. The after tax return of 11.1 percent earned by the deposit-taking sector fell short of the return of 12.2 percent for all industry, the 13.7 percent for non-financial industry, and the 22.3 percent for all services. Overall, the after tax return for deposit-taking ranked last in the eight major sectors, but by a smaller margin than for before tax profits.

As with the before tax comparisons, considerable differences exist with respect to the after tax profits of the components of the deposit-taking sector. On average, the chartered banks earned 11.4 percent compared to 8 percent for the loan companies and 7.5 percent for the trust companies. These lower returns for the two subgroups put them behind all the major sectors with respect to after tax rate of profit. Still, the improvement for the banks was only sufficient to place them ahead of utilities among the major sectors.

The profit performance for the deposit-taking sector for the years 1977 to 1984 appears substantially different than that found by Mintz for the chartered banks during the years 1968 to 1973. Throughout this recent period, deposit-taking institutions ranked at the bottom of major industries with respect to before tax profits. This result would be expected in a competitive market because of the lower effective tax rates that apply to the deposit-taking sector. Nevertheless, on an after tax basis the deposit-taking sector still ranked last out of eight major sectors.

These data suggest that the profit performance of the deposit-taking sector as a whole could be characterized as subnormal. Any judgement should be tempered with caution for a number of reasons. Closer examination of the data suggest that the overall results have been heavily influenced by the early years of the comparison where the non-financial sector outperformed the deposit-taking sector, frequently by a substantial margin. In contrast, the deposit-taking sector earned a higher rate of accounting profit than the non-financial industry over two of the last three years. In addition, as will be discussed more fully below, accounting data may be unreliable as an indicator of industry performance in times of inflation such as characterized the period of review.

Return to Shareholders

An alternative measure of the return is the return realized by the shareholders of firms in a sector. For the purpose of this study, monthly data were gathered for the return index for the Toronto Stock Exchange 300 Index (TSE 300), and the bank and trust and loan subindexes over the period from January

Table 30

Annual Returns to Shareholders: Banks, Trust and Savings, and TSE 300

	Banks	Trust & Savings	TSE 300
1980	31.33	20.90	14.23
1981	-13.86	-3.60	-16.35
1982	27.54	39.88	19.74
1983	27.52	64.55	26.32
1984	7.39	27.88	9.08
1985	18.34	24.03	13.36
1986	27.32	35.36	21.39
Average	14.61	24.47	10.16

Source: Toronto Stock Exchange Review.
Note: These returns are calculated from January to January Return Index values.

1978 to December 1986. These return indexes, as distinct from the TSE price indexes, measure the total returns to an investor from holding a stock, including dividends and stock splits.

The returns to shareholders from holding shares in banks and trust and savings firms are compared in table 30 with the return earned by holders of a portfolio representative of the TSE 300. As can be seen, the returns to shareholders in the two groups from the deposit-taking sector exceed those to shareholders of the TSE 300 by a substantial margin, especially in the case of the trust and savings. More remarkable is the consistency of this superior performance. In every year of the sample, trust and savings outperformed the TSE 300, and in every year but one the bank subindex outperformed the index.

Returns: A Summary

The two sets of return data comparing the returns of the deposit-taking sector to the rest of the economy present a substantial paradox. On the basis of accounting returns, the deposit-taking sector ranks last among major sectors, whereas by stock market returns the two components of the deposit-taking sector outperformed the TSE 300 (a measure representative of the whole economy) by a substantial margin.

A complete analysis of these differences is well beyond the scope of this study. Nevertheless, several possible contributing factors can be suggested. First, the firms listed in the TSE 300 may not be representative of the industry subgroups. The TSE 300 includes large banks and trust companies but does not cover the smaller banks and trust companies that have failed or have been forced to merge through the threat of failure. While undoubtedly a contributing element, this factor cannot explain very much of the difference because these smaller institutions would only be weighted by their size in the accounting returns.

A second factor that may explain the difference between the measures of return has been the rapid inflation that characterized many of the years for which data are reported in table 29. Commenting on an earlier period of inflation, Glenn Jenkins stated that "inflation has caused a substantial decrease in the current income of non-financial businesses in Canada...Inflation has had a very different impact on the financial sector as compared to manufacturing and non-manufacturing....the total impact of inflation has been to transfer income toward the financial sector in Canada" (1977:48). These distortions for non-financial industry do not show up in accounting income; instead, accounting profits overstate actual profits adjusted for the effects of inflation. While the extent of this bias could not be determined without a detailed analysis, its presence is given some credence by the fact that the excess of the accounting returns of the non-financial sector over the deposit-taking sector was greatest in the earlier years when the rate of inflation was higher.

This discussion has suggested some of the factors that may have accounted for the performance of the deposit-taking sector relative to other sectors with respect to the two measures of return that have been presented. Until the importance of these and other possible factors has been determined, the difference between accounting and market measures of the relative return of the deposit-taking sector remains a puzzle.

VARIABILITY OF PROFITS

The variability of profits provides a further measure of an industry's performance by indicating the risk involved in investing in that industry. Generally, it is argued that higher than normal profits must be sustained in an industry that is riskier than the rest of the economy in order to attract capital to that industry.

The variability of profit in an industry will be measured in two ways in this study. The first measure, presented earlier in table 29, shows the variability of accounting rates of return on a year-to-year basis as measured by the standard deviation of annual returns. The second measure, one suggested by the modern theory of finance, is beta, which indicates the sensitivity of the returns earned from holding a firm's or industry's stock to changes in the return earned by investors in the market at large.

The use of the simple standard deviation as a measure of risk assumes that all risk is the same in the view of investors. The use of beta, on the other hand, assumes that risk can be divided into two types, diversifiable and non-diversifiable, that are viewed differently by investors. Investors do not require compensation to undertake diversifiable risk because it tends toward an expected value of zero with a sufficiently large portfolio. Undiversifiable risk, on the other hand, reflects the common elements influencing returns in the market and cannot be eliminated by holding a diversified portfolio.

Beta measures the sensitivity of securities with respect to the common market influences. A beta equal to unity means that a security responds on a one-to-one basis to movements in the market return. A beta less than unity means it responds less than proportionately to the market factor. And a return greater than unity means it responds more than proportionately. Investors, according to the modern theory of finance, require higher returns to be willing to hold securities with higher betas.

Simple Variability

The standard deviation for the accounting return of the deposit-taking sector as shown in table 29 for the years 1976 to 1984 was 3.6 percent for before tax return and 1.9 percent for after tax.[2] On a before tax basis, the variability of the return of the deposit-taking sector was less than that for all industry and for non-financial industry and ranked fifth out of eight major industries behind mining, manufacturing, wholesale trade, agriculture, forestry and fisheries, and ahead of only construction, retail trade and utilities. On an after tax basis, the variability of the returns of the deposit-taking sector was lower than all sectors other than utilities.

Beta

The calculation of beta requires the same data on the returns earned by shareholders discussed above. Beta can be determined for a security i by estimating an equation:

$$r(i) = A(i) + B(i) \, rm$$

where $r(i)$ is the return on the ith security; rm, the return on the market portfolio; $A(i)$, a coefficient A for the ith security; and $B(i)$, the beta of the ith security. The results from this equation for the banks and for the trust and savings sector are presented in table 31.

The results presented in table 31 are consistent with those derived from the simple variability analysis above. The holders of bank shares experience a 0.74 percent change in their return, and the holders of trust and savings shares

Table 31
The Beta Measure of Return Variability
Bank and Trust and Savings Subindexes, 1978 to 1986

Banks:

$$dlnB = A + B(dln\ 300)$$

variable	coefficient	standard error	t value
constant	.00539	.00469	1.150
(dlnB)	.741	.0885	8.371
RSQ(adj)	.457		
F = 70.1	(1,81 DF)		

Trust and Savings:

$$dTSL = a + b(dln\ TSL)$$

variable	coefficient	standard error	t value
constant	.0150	.00586	2.55
(dlnTSL)	.692	.111	6.255
RSQ(adj)	.318		
F = 39.1	(1,81 DF)		

Source: *Toronto Stock Exchange Review*, various issues.

Notes: dlnB = change in ln of bank return index.
dlnTSL = change in ln of trust and saving return index.
dln300 = change in ln of Toronto 300 returns index.
RSQ(adj) = coefficient of determination adjusted for
degrees of freedom.

experience a 0.69 percent change in their return for every 1 percent change
in the return in the TSE 300 return index. These results indicate that the
shares of banks and trust and savings companies are substantially less
volatile in their response to the market than the shares that make up the TSE
300 index.

Variability: A Summary

Evidence on the variability of the returns to the deposit-taking sector has
been derived from both simple measures of variability and the more sophisticated beta analysis. Unlike the analysis of returns, the results from the
variability analysis are consistent: the deposit-taking sector appears to be less
risky than the rest of the economy.

COSTS OF DEPOSIT-TAKING INSTITUTIONS

Comparison of the costs of deposit-taking institutions with those of other enterprises creates a number of difficulties. The appropriate measure of expenses for deposit-taking institutions depends on the perspective from which they are viewed. If they are viewed as identical to other enterprises, their revenues including interest received would be treated as sales, and all costs including all interest paid would be considered as expenses in earning that revenue. The approach taken in chapters 2 and 3 suggests that deposit-taking institutions produce the service of intermediation and that the spread between interest rates paid and received represent a major part of the revenues from that service. In this case, the appropriate measure of their costs would be the total expenses less the interest paid to depositors. According to the pass-through approach to the measurement of the product of deposit-taking institutions, this interest is attributed in the first instance to the ultimate lenders.

Table 32 compares the costs of deposit-taking institutions with the costs of other services, non-financial industry and all industry. As can be seen, other interest is by far the major expense for deposit-taking institutions in the conventional accounting statements of their income and expense, making up 73 percent of total expenses as compared to 3 percent for services and non-financial industry and 7 percent for all industry including the deposit-taking sector itself. All other differences are swamped by this difference in other interest.

The data in table 30 have been adjusted to correspond to the view that deposit-taking institutions supply intermediary services. For the purpose of comparability, other interest has been excluded from the expenses of all sectors. From this perspective, substantial differences appear between the costs of intermediaries and other enterprises. The most marked difference occurs with respect to materials. Deposit-taking institutions did not record any expenses for materials, whereas service enterprises spend almost 20 percent; all industry 58 percent, and non-financial industry 59 percent. This difference in materials expense almost dominates all other differences in expenses. Deposit-taking institutions spend more than non-financial enterprises on every category except repair and maintenance, royalties, mortgage interest, direct taxes, depreciation, and depletion.

This comparison takes into account only those expenditures incurred by deposit-taking institutions in producing their value added. A similar adjustment could be made to other industries by excluding expenditures for material from their expenses on the basis of the same reasoning. On this basis, a number of the differences between deposit-taking and other sectors disappear or are reversed. After this adjustment, the service sector spends more than the deposit-taking sector on salaries and wages, and the differen-

Table 32
The Cost Structure of Deposit-Taking Institutions, 1984

	Deposit-Taking Institutions	Services	All Industries	Non-Financial Industries
Total revenue	49641	54558	866393	769282
Other interest	34780	1360	58113	14118
Total revenue less other interest	14861	53198	808280	

	Deposit-Taking Institutions	Percent of expenses less other interest	Services	Percent of expenses less other interest	All Industries	Percent of expenses less other interest	Percent of expenses less other interest and materials	Non-Financial Industries	Percent of expenses less other interest	Percent of expenses less other interest and materials
Materials		0.000	9647	0.195	436095	0.578	0.419	431208	0.605	0.437
Salaries and wages	4875	0.376	16380	0.331	133450	0.177	0.419	122892	0.173	0.026
Repair and maintenance	81	0.006	769	0.016	7916	0.010	0.025	7242	0.010	0.027
Rent (real estate)	362	0.028	1690	0.034	8561	0.011	0.027	7559	0.011	0.009
Rent (other)	51	0.004	388	0.008	2623	0.003	0.008	2533	0.004	0.025
Royalties		0.000	172	0.003	7094	0.009	0.022	7069	0.010	0.029
Bond interest	1140	0.088	120	0.002	10241	0.014	0.032	8121	0.011	0.004
Mortgage interest	14	0.001	366	0.007	4187	0.006	0.013	1067	0.001	0.013
Taxes other than direct taxes	68	0.005	471	0.010	44943	0.060	0.141	3545	0.005	0.074
Depreciation	331	0.026	2544	0.051	22532	0.030	0.071	20685	0.029	-0.009
Depletion and amortization	11	0.001	1	0.000	2482	0.003	0.008	2452	0.003	0.348
Other expenses	6040	0.466	16917	0.342	114803	0.152	0.360	97872	0.137	
Total expenses	47744		50826		813038			726361		
Total expenses less other interest	12964	1.000	49466	1.000	754925	1.000		712184	1.000	
Total expenses less other interest and materials					318830		1.000	280976		1.000

Source: Statistics Canada, Corporate Financial Statistics.

ces become more pronounced with respect to repairs and maintenance, rent and depreciation among major items. The adjustment also reverses the expenditures on salaries and wages for the deposit-taking sector relative to the non-financial sector. Salaries and wages account for 42 percent of expenses in the non-financial sector compared to only 38 percent in the deposit-taking sector. The only major categories for which the proportion of expenses in the deposit-taking sector exceeded that for non-financial industry are bond interest and other expenses.

In summary, it is difficult to make a comparison of the costs of the deposit-taking industry with the rest of the economy because of the differences in the nature of the activities. In terms of overall expenses, deposit-taking institutions spend much more on interest expense and much less on materials than other industries. When costs are adjusted to reflect the expenses of producing value added, these vast differences disappear. Non-financial industry spends a larger proportion of its total expenses on salaries and wages, rent, indirect taxes and depreciation than does the deposit-taking sector.

NOTES

1. These data differ substantially from those presented in the Selected Corporate Ratios in *Corporate Financial Statistics*. The data differ in that those used in the Selected Corporate Ratios express the rate of return as a ratio of "net profit before taxes and non recurring items" to the sum "due to shareholders and affiliates" and "total equity." This procedure would appear to understate that rate of return by omitting the interest paid to shareholders and affiliates from the numerator while including the debt in the denominator.

2. The components of the deposit-taking industry consistently had higher standard deviations than the industry as a whole. While this result may initially appear surprising, some of the fluctuations of the individual sectors apparently offset each other on a year-to-year basis.

Chapter 7

INNOVATION IN THE DEPOSIT-TAKING SECTOR

The dominating feature of the deposit-taking sector in recent years has been the extent and pace of innovation. While the basic services offered to customers remain unchanged, their forms and the ways in which they are offered have been dramatically transformed. The purpose of this chapter is to analyse the impact of innovation on the functioning of the deposit-taking sector.

SOURCES OF INNOVATION

After many years of research by economists, the process of innovation in the production of goods and services remains poorly understood. Research on innovation in financial services has been more recent and has not experienced any greater success. Still, the significance of innovation in the deposit-taking sector means that it is important to try to understand the sources and consequences of innovation. Such an understanding can prevent the adoption of public policies that would unnecessarily impede innovation that contributes to the productivity of the financial industry. At the same time, it must be recognized that not all innovation need be socially productive.

Silber (1975), one of the few economists to study the process of innovation in the financial sector, argues that financial firms, like other firms, will seek out innovations in response to changes that either reduce profits or enhance the possibility of profits by expanding the choices available to the firm. Such changes occur continually, but innovations are relatively rare. Silber goes on to argue that innovation will be the response only when the changes are perceived as abnormal and the normal responses of the firm are found to be inadequate.

The "constrained optimization" of the firm is limited by the environment facing the firm. That is in turn determined by economic conditions, the regulations governing the actions of the firm, the technology available, and the state of knowledge concerning the alternatives available to the firm. Innovation can be stimulated by changes in any of these variables.

Economic Conditions

Changes in economic conditions have recently been an important stimulus to innovation in the financial sector. The unprecedented inflation of the 1970s and 1980s has made traditional financial instruments inappropriate for the needs of borrowers and lenders. Among the new instruments that have been developed as a response to inflation have been floating rate business loans and floating rate mortgages.

The economic conditions that lead to innovation in the deposit-taking industry can be either transitory or permanent. Clearly, the current costs of transitory economic conditions must be more substantial than more permanent conditions before they would induce the same amount of innovation, particularly as any benefits from the innovation can be expected to persist only as long as its cause. In some instances, an innovation instigated in response to transitory conditions may continue to yield benefits even after the transitory conditions have disappeared. One example of such an innovation has been the sophisticated systems of cash management that emerged as a response to the high interest rates of the 1970s but that remained after the high interest rates abated.

Regulation

The financial industry represents one of the most heavily regulated sectors in capitalist economies. Regulations constrain the choices available to financial firms to those alternatives permitted in the regulatory framework. Profitable opportunities are created for firms to find ways of conducting business that permit them to do things that are otherwise precluded by regulation. Perhaps the most outstanding example of an innovation that has been induced by regulation can be found in the development of the Eurodollar market. First, foreign banks and, subsequently, American banks used the Eurodollar market to perform transactions on terms that were not permitted in the United States because of regulation. In particular, Eurodollar transactions avoided the reserve requirements, the interest withholding taxes, and the ceilings under Regulation Q to the interest rates that could be paid on deposits.

The importance of regulation as a determinant of innovation differs substantially between the United States and Canada because of the systems of regulation in the two countries. Banks in the United States have been subject to limitations on the interest rates they can pay and to restrictions on the number and location of their branch offices. Many important innovations in that country have been directed to overcoming these restrictions. For example, the growth of NOW (negotiated order of withdrawal) accounts and money market mutual funds both were responses by financial institutions to avoid the prohibition against the payment of interest on demand deposits. Similarly, the earlier development of drive-in banking in the United States reflected an attempt to overcome the limits on branching by making existing branches more accessible to a broader group of customers. A bank might resort to opening a drive-in branch between two shopping centres because of a limitation on its branches. In Canada, a bank in the same circumstances would have the option of opening a branch in each shopping centre.

Technology

Much of the payments and intermediary functions of deposit-taking institutions consists of the processing, transfer and storage of information. As a result, changes in the technology of the communications and data processing industries have served to stimulate innovation in the financial sector in much the same way as in many other sectors. Technological change permits firms to perform the same services more cheaply or to provide the services in new ways not previously possible. Developments in communications and computer technology have been among the most important forces leading to change in the financial sector in recent years.

The State of Knowledge

The final source of innovation is the state of knowledge of the constraints facing the financial firm and its customers. Many advances in financial instruments have incorporated advances in knowledge that are not embodied in any form of equipment. For example, financial institutions are now beginning to offer their customers financial instruments that protect them against undesirable movements in interest rates paid or received. This protection has been made possible by the ability to interpret these interest caps or floors as financial options and to use option pricing theory to determine the appropriate price for such features. In addition, this interpretation of option theory permits the financial institution to determine the position in the option market that would permit it to offset the risks in providing the guarantees to its customers.

TYPES OF INNOVATIONS

Innovations can be classified according to the way in which they influence the firms that introduce them. Process innovations alter the ways in which firms produce their product and have little influence on the nature of the product. The benefits to customers from process innovations come from the downward pressures on prices caused by the reduced costs resulting from the innovation. Product innovations, in contrast, change the product produced by the firm. Customers benefit from product innovations through the improved quality of the product in terms of their demands. The benefits from product innovation are much more difficult to measure than are those from process innovation. As discussed earlier, an important element of the quality of financial services is the time required from the user to gain the benefits of these services. Any complete accounting of the benefits of product innovation must take into account the time saved for, or the additional time required from, the customer.

INNOVATION IN DEPOSIT-TAKING: THE CANADIAN EXPERIENCE

The deposit-taking sector experienced a remarkable, and indeed an unprecedented, clustering of innovations from the mid-1960s through the 1980s. Moreover, it seems likely that the process will continue, though possibly abated somewhat, for some time in the future. The major innovations that have contributed to change in the deposit-taking sector are summarized in table 33. In order to understand how these innovations have changed and will continue to change the deposit-taking sector, their causes and consequences will be discussed individually in the remainder of this section.

MICR Encoding of Cheques

The initial use by Canadian banks in 1962 of magnetic ink character recognition (MICR) encoding for cheques was important in two respects. First, as will be discussed below, it permitted a change in the processing of cheques that has resulted in cost savings for the banks. Secondly, and more significantly, MICR represented the first in a series of innovations that have continued in rapid succession to the present.

MICR encoding consists of machine readable symbols in a standard language imprinted on the face of cheques that enabled the banks to switch from

Table 33

Major Innovations in the Deposit-Taking Sector

Year	Technological Innovation
1960	MICR Encoding
	Batch Processing
1965	Online Systems
	Bank Cards
	Cash Dispensers
1970	Automated Banking Machines
1975	Multi-Branch Banking
	Daily Interest Savings Accounts
	Direct Deposit/Tape Exchange
1982	Pre-authorized Payments
	Credit Union Debit Cards
1984	ABM Sharing

Source: The Canadian Bankers' Association.

manual to machine sorting of cheques. The adoption of MICR encoding was primarily a process innovation in that the product offered by the banks was virtually unchanged and the benefits to the banks flowed entirely in the form of reduced costs. Binhammer and Williams (1976) estimate that while the clearing of an MICR encoded cheque in 1976 was around 13 cents, the clearing of a cheque that was not encoded and had to be handled manually cost at least three times as much. From their introduction in 1962, the use of MICR encoded cheques grew in ten years to account for over 90 percent of all cheques. By the mid-1980s the use of MICR cheques had become so pervasive that extra charges are made to customers for the processing of unencoded cheques.

The adoption of MICR encoding has altered the structure of the deposit-taking sector in two important respects. First, the encoded cheques permitted deposit-taking institutions other than banks to participate more fully in the cheque clearing system. Prior to encoding, these institutions had to route their cheques through a designated branch of a chartered bank. In effect, the accounts of these institutions were treated for clearing purposes like the accounts of any other customer. If the deposit-taking institution shifted to another bank, its cheques would have to be changed to indicate the change in its clearing agent. The MICR technology permitted these other deposit-taking institutions to have their own identifying codes. As a result, if one of these institutions switched its clearing agent, its cheques could remain unchanged and only the routing instructions in the cheque processing equipment would need to be altered.

Secondly, MICR encoding had a substantial effect on the internal organization of banks and other financial institutions. Prior to MICR, preliminary sorting of cheques took place at the branch level. Subsequently, As Binhammer and Williams report, "except at branches away from the urban centres, very little cheque sorting of accounting remains at the branch level of the chartered banks. Cheques and other vouchers are now picked up from the branches by courier after branch closing time and taken to data centres for overnight batch-processing. Processed items, together with various reports, are returned to the branches on the following morning" (1976:117-18).

Overall, the change to MICR encoding would be expected to reduce the number of clerical employees overall, with a parallel shift of the remaining clerical employment away from the branch and toward the regional processing centres.

Bank Cards

Bank cards were introduced in Canada in 1968 when Bank Canadian National, Canadian Bank of Commerce, Royal Bank of Canada and Toronto-Dominion Bank jointly introduced Bank Americard in Canada as Chargex (now Visa). Subsequently, in 1973, the Bank of Montreal and the Provincial Bank jointly offered Mastercharge to their customers. The growth in the use of bank cards since their introduction is illustrated by the summary statistics presented in table 34. As can be seen, at the end of 1985, 14 million cards were in circulation with average annual sales of almost $1,400 per card. In terms of the payments system overall, bank cards were used for 373 million transactions compared to the 1,678 million cheques processed. In value terms, bank card transactions were less significant, accounting for only $20 billion compared to the $9,101 billion for cheques. The importance of bank cards is probably understated by the statistics on gross dollar volume. Bank cards are used solely for retail transactions, whereas cheques are used for a wider variety of transactions including inter-firm and intergovernmental transfers that involve huge sums in one transaction.

Table 34

Selected Statistics on Bank Credit Cards

Year	Number of Cards (millions)	Dollar Sales (billions)	Transactions (millions)	Merchant Accounts(1) (thousands)
1977	8.2	3.6	119	271
1978	9.0	4.9	151	291
1979	9.9	6.6	185	322
1980	10.8	8.8	218	347
1981	12.0	10.6	250	372
1982	11.6	13.8	275	382
1983	12.1	14.8	298	420
1984	13.1	16.9	325	443
1985	14.0	19.4	373	527

Source: Canadian Bankers' Association.

Note: (1) Includes duplication merchants who accept both Mastercard and Visa.

The development of the bank card was dependent in large degree on technological developments. The acceptance of the card for larger transactions requires the merchant to gain approval, either direct or indirect, from the bank that issued the card. This approval process requires a link between the merchants and ultimately the issuing bank. At the first level, the merchant contacts the authorization point through a phone call or through a "dial up point of sale terminal" that links directly with a computer. In Canada, these authorization points are centralized with most banks having only one. Communication links are required between the authorization centres of different issuing institutions, both domestically and internationally. Cheap communications have clearly been an essential element in the development and evolution of the bank card.

Deposit-taking institutions gain revenue from issuing the cards in a number of ways. Consumers using the cards may pay an annual fee for the service, a charge per transaction, or both. The annual fee varies with the services available from the card and can range from $12 to around $100 per annum. Consumers who use the credit available through the card must pay interest at a rate above the typical consumer credit rate charged by deposit-taking institutions. In addition, merchants that accept credit cards must pay a fee of from 1.5 to 5 percent of the value of each transaction.

Bank cards, in contrast to MICR encoding, have vastly changed the nature of the product offered to bank customers. Prior to their emergence, the typical consumer was restricted to making retail purchases with either cash or the presentation of a personal cheque. The use of cash was inconvenient because of security problems for large sums and the need to anticipate expenditures in advance so as to have sufficient cash available. The use of cheques was restricted to purchases where the seller could be assured, generally by personal knowledge of the customer, that the cheque would be honoured. The alternative of using charge accounts or travel and entertainment cards was available only to more affluent consumers.

The technology of bank cards benefits consumers mainly through the saving of time and through increased convenience. In everyday transactions, the consumer is able to reduce the frequency of trips to the bank, knowing that the bank card can be used for many types of transactions. For travellers, the benefits from bank cards can be even more substantial in that they permit payments for transactions where cash would be very inconvenient and the use of cheques unacceptable. In addition, bank cards reduce the need for separate foreign exchange transactions when the customer is travelling abroad.

The use of bank cards can be thought of as a logical evolution of the use of cheques with three notable differences: the guarantee of the card issuer gives the card greater acceptability than cheques; consumers make payments by increasing their outstanding credit rather than running down deposit balances as they would by using cheques; and consumer accounts are centralized rather than being identified with branches. The first two make little difference for the organization of the deposit-taking industry aside from the fact that institutions offering card services to their customers may find it necessary to make some form of association with other institutions to give their customers the fullest benefits of the card. The last characteristic, centralization of the administrative function, de-emphasizes the role of the local branch and gives deposit-taking institutions the option of locating their card processing facilities on the basis of factors other than proximity to their customers.

Automated Banking Machines

Automated banking machines (ABMs) are the descendants of cash dispensers which were introduced in Canada around 1969. The original generation of cash dispensers were limited to giving customers fixed amounts of cash and were often offline.[1] A new generation of sophisticated ABMs emerged in 1972 that were said "to be able to perform up to 95 per cent of the transactions that were performed by a human teller" (Binhammer and Williams, p. 95). While the initial ABMs were offline, located in branches, and limited to the customers of that institution, ABMs can now be found in many locations away from bank branches such as airports and grocery stores. They are typically online and can be used through co-operative arrangements by

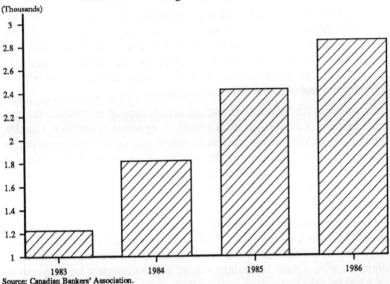

Figure 4
Automated Banking Machines at Chartered Banks

Source: Canadian Bankers' Association.

customers of many different deposit-taking institutions. Most customers are able to use ABMs anywhere in Canada or the United States and some are able to use cash machines in many countries in Europe and Asia with cards issued by Canadian institutions.

The spread of ABMs was initially fairly slow. In the two years after their introduction in 1972, only a total of 24 machines had been installed by Canadian banks (Binhammer and Williams 1976). For a long time, many bankers and others believed that a lack of consumer acceptance would limit the use of ABMs. The data presented in figure 4 suggest that their views were unduly pessimistic. By 1986, the chartered banks alone had installed over 2,800 ABMs, with over half installed between 1983 and 1986. As of July 1984, trust companies had installed 90 ABMs, and credit unions another 416 ABMs.

The development of the services of the ABM has been very dependent on the state of communication and computer technology. Computer technology was needed in offline installations in order to read the information on the customer's card, determine whether the required transaction was admissible, and carry out the transaction. Online ABMs must be able to communicate with a central computer, or in many cases a network of central computers, in order to carry out the customer's transaction.

The ABM, like the bank card, must be viewed as a product innovation. The ABM changed the nature of banking by allowing customers to gain services at locations removed from their bank branches and at times outside normal banking hours. The benefits accrue in the form of increased convenience; customers are able to perform their banking transactions in ways that are less costly to them.

The charges for transactions through ABMs depend on whether the customer carries out the transaction at a machine operated by his bank. Usually, transactions at ABMs are treated as normal transactions when the customer uses the machines at his own institution. Charges are generally one dollar for transactions at other institutions and two dollars for transactions outside Canada. Some institutions have used lower charges on ABM transactions as a competitive device.

The development of the ABM has a great potential to change the organization of the deposit-taking sector. The ABM reduces the customer's need to be present at a branch office in order to carry out banking transactions. Moreover, as is already becoming evident, the smaller space requirements of the ABM permits institutions to place them in locations where the rent for a branch would be prohibitive. As these developments continue, the role of the branch will be transformed from a place where many routine and few complicated or unusual transactions take place to one confined to special transactions beyond the capacity of ABMs. Branches will still be needed for negotiating lines of credit for consumers and for many services for business customers.

The de-emphasis of the branch affects the distribution of employment in the deposit-taking sector in much the same way as the bank card. First, the mix of employees can be expected to shift away from the tellers and clerical employees associated with the transactions identified with branches. A need will be created for more highly skilled employees to operate the computers and communications equipment that control the network of ABMs. The employees remaining at the branches are also likely to possess a high level of expertise so that they can deal with the more complicated transactions that will be dealt with at branches.

Daily Interest Accounts

Traditionally, banks and other financial institutions paid interest to their customers on the basis of the minimum balance held in savings accounts over some period, usually a month. This practice worked to the disadvantage of customers with balances that fluctuate inasmuch as they would receive interest on only a small portion of their average balance over the period and was regarded by many to be inequitable. The introduction of daily interest saving accounts permitted the customer to earn interest on some funds over periods of less than a month before transferring them as needed to their chequing accounts. Subsequently, the daily interest savings chequing account combined chequing privileges and daily interest in the same account.

The daily interest accounts have developed as a consequence of a number of different factors. The presence of high interest rates resulting from inflation meant that households were suffering losses of substantial interest through holding non-interest bearing accounts or accounts paying interest on minimum balances. The offering of daily interest accounts was facilitated greatly by the adoption of computer technology which made the extensive computations feasible. Indeed, the Canadian government had threatened on a number of occasions in the 1970s to legislate payment of daily interest only to be met with the argument that such a practice would be prohibitively expensive with the nationwide branching system (Landy 1980). As was the case with many innovations offered to consumers, the daily interest accounts were initially offered by smaller institutions such as credit unions and trust companies before they were offered by the chartered banks.

Table 35
Daily Interest Accounts at Chartered Banks
(in billions of dollars)

| End of Year | Chequable Savings Accounts | | Non-Chequable Savings Accounts | |
	Daily Interest	Other	Daily Interest	Other
1979	—	6.8	1.0	27.5
1980	—	7.0	4.0	33.8
1981	—	6.1	6.8	35.5
1982	1.7	5.2	9.5	38.3
1983	3.4	5.3	11.0	39.9
1984	9.7	4.9	9.9	35.6
1985	21.8	4.6	10.8	31.1
1986	28.4	4.4	17.0	26.7

Source: *Bank of Canada Review*, various issues.

The use of daily interest accounts at chartered banks is shown in table 35. As can be seen, the daily interest savings had grown to about one-sixth of non-chequable savings accounts from their introduction in September 1979 to the introduction of daily interest chequing accounts in July 1982. The most significant growth in daily interest accounts, however, has taken place in the chequable accounts where daily interest accounts now comprise 80 percent of the total.

The main implications of the daily interest accounts have to do with the ability of deposit-taking institutions to compete with other forms of investment for the consumer's funds. Now, with the daily interest feature, consumers can gain the benefit of higher interest rates without the need to manage their funds among different types of accounts. Like the other product innovations, the daily interest accounts improve the product available to consumers for the same expenditure of their labour or provide the same product with a reduction in the labour requirements. Daily interest accounts have, however, necessitated adjustments in the pricing practices followed by financial institutions. Prior to the introduction of daily interest accounts, many bank services were supplied without charge as an implicit offset to the low rate of interest. The introduction of daily interest accounts has forced the financial institutions to charge fees for a wider range of services. Finally, in contrast to other innovations such as the ABM, the daily interest account will not affect the organization of deposit-taking firms. The daily interest account itself was the outcome of opportunities provided by the adoption of computer technology.

Securitization

The term "securitization" refers to a group of new practices of banks and other deposit-taking institutions that primarily affect their larger corporate customers and can be defined as "the process by which traditional bank or thrift institution assets, mainly loans or mortgages, are converted into negotiable securities which may be purchased either by depository institutions or by non-bank investors" (B.I.S. 1986). Unlike most of the innovations discussed to this point that have been dependent on the advances in either communications or computer technology, securitization has been the result of a combination of regulatory and real economic factors.

The pressures for securitization on the regulatory side have been caused by the increasing concern by regulators with the capital position of banks and other deposit-taking institutions. By securitizing loans, financial institutions are able to play a role in arranging credit for their customers without at the same time being committed to holding the resulting claim through the term of the loan. Economic pressures for securitization have also resulted from the problem loans that many deposit-taking institutions have made to developing countries and to troubled domestic sectors such as agriculture and energy. To the extent that these problem loans have lowered the credit ratings of deposit institutions, the advantages of bank loans relative to other forms of finance have been reduced for firms with high credit ratings. They are able to offer their own securities to direct lenders on relatively advantageous terms, with or without the guarantee of their bank.

Securitization raises one important policy issue for bank regulation. Intermediation, through simultaneous lending and borrowing, adds to the overall size of a bank's balance sheet and, accordingly, increases its need for capital. Bank regulation in Canada has increased its emphasis on capital adequacy in recent years. Securitization, when a bank guarantee is involved, leads to the same need for additional capital in order for the bank to meet its commitments, but this need for capital may not be as apparent because the transaction occurs only "off balance sheet." Regulators must, as a result, ensure that the new financing techniques are adequately reflected in the regulatory framework governing financial institutions.

New Financial Instruments

Many new financial instruments have been created by financial institutions from the 1970s onward. The choice for consumers of interest paid on a daily basis on their savings accounts has been discussed above. Similarly, business can borrow through instruments with floating interest rates, arrange swaps between currencies and interest rates with respect to the terms for loans, and even protect themselves against unfavourable interest movements through caps and floors. Home buyers can arrange mortgages on a variety of terms with respect to maturity and interest rate.

The development of new instruments on the lending side of the business of intermediaries reflects similar influences to the developments on the deposit side. Common factors in both sets of developments have been the high and uncertain interest rates of the late 1970s onward. Some of these instruments prevent borrowers from being "locked into" loans on unfavourable terms, though at the expense of bearing the risks of further interest movements. The interest and currency swap loans permit firms to tailor loans to meet their needs with respect to the terms of interest payments or currency of payment. The role of technological change, however, was not as crucial as in the case of the main innovation on the deposit side, daily interest deposits.

The interest caps on loans are one innovation that appears to have been made possible through both academic and technological developments. The modern theory of option pricing enabled financial institutions to determine the appropriate terms for options that protect lenders or borrowers from interest rate risks beyond certain limits, whereas computer technology provided a means for determining the appropriate price of the option. Although interest caps and floors are now just beginning to be offered to bank customers, they appear to bring back the role of financial institutions in protecting their customers from risk. Regulators, however, will be required to study the implications of interest caps and floors for the risk borne by the deposit-taking institutions and take these risks into account in their regulation. Since many of these risks may be offsetting, any regulations should be based on the net overall risks borne by financial institutions as a result of these instruments.

Cost Saving Measures

A number of changes in procedures have been introduced by the deposit-taking institutions during the 1970s for the purposes of reducing costs. Foremost among these measures has been the "truncation" of the paper flows documenting cheque payments and credit card transactions. Truncation refers to a process in which the transfer of paper documentation is stopped at an early stage in the process and its information is transferred subsequently by electronic means. The paper documentation is stored at the first stage to provide verification for the information that is transmitted electronically.

The savings through truncation result from the reduced need to transfer paper through the system. These savings have come at some costs to customers. Truncation necessarily reduces the information flow to customers. Instead of receiving cancelled cheques and duplicates of sales slips, customers now receive only summary statements. Some customers will find that the summary information will be adequate for their purposes, whereas others will be inconvenienced by the loss of information. For these customers, truncation will be the opposite of some of the innovations discussed earlier that improve the quality of banking services. For them, truncation results in a deterioration of quality.

Point of Sale Terminals

The slower than expected introduction of ABMs should lend caution to any attempt to forecast the next innovations in the deposit-taking sector. This caution aside, the widespread use of point of sale (POS) terminals appears likely in the near future. As in the case of the ABM, this timing appears unduly delayed in light of predictions of an imminent banking revolution that were being made in the 1970s. Still, POS terminals share with ABMs the need for customers to accept new ways of doing their financial business. The apparent acceptance of ABMs by a significant proportion of customers suggests that one obstacle to their use has been overcome.

The POS terminal provides a means by which customers can pay merchants by activating an electronic transfer of funds from their accounts at deposit-taking institutions to the merchant's account. To an extent the transaction would resemble a credit card transaction because prior authorization would be required from the payer's deposit-taking institution. The transaction differs because the payment takes place instantaneously and is drawn from the customer's deposit. The necessary elements of the POS technology are already in place. It has similar needs to the sophisticated ABM—cheap communications and computers to verify and implement the transfer.

The use of POS terminals for making payments will add to the pressures de-emphasizing the role of the branch. In particular, it will reduce the needs for cash in making retail transactions and consequently reduce the frequency at which consumers and retailers withdraw and deposit cash.

Agreement on the organization of the POS payments system remains as an obstacle to its development, though some elements are clear. Communication will be required between merchants and institutions from which consumers make their payments. In addition, agreement will be necessary with respect to the standards adopted in the payments process. Both these matters appear to have been resolved in the present authorization procedures for credit card transactions and in the interchange arrangements for the use of ABMs.

More contentious will be the issue of the ownership of the POS network and its components. In particular, would the ownership of POS equipment by retailers violate the standards required for participation in the payments system? Two separate arguments appear to be involved. First, participation in a co-operative venture such as the existing payments system requires adherence by its members to a standard code of procedures. For example, members must agree on the obligations and rights of institutions for dealing with n.s.f. cheques. What are the time limitations for return? How soon must compensation be made? Can the cheque be resubmitted? This aspect of the POS system appears to be uncontroversial with respect to ownership. Participating retailers will have to accept whatever code emerges regardless of whether they own the terminals.

The important issue then appears to be whether the ownership of POS terminals jeopardizes some desirable feature of the payments system. The present separation of the payments system from other activities is based on a need for the safety of the deposits used for making payments and the argument that this safety might be risked by combining the supply of payments with other economic activities. If this is the argument, the ownership of terminals would not appear to be an issue. POS terminals are a device for transferring payments, the ownership of these devices can be completely independent from the supply of chequable deposits.

INNOVATION IN PERSPECTIVE

The survey of innovation in the deposit-taking sector has by necessity been selective. The innovations that have been discussed show the entire range in terms of how they have affected customers and the deposit-taking institutions themselves. Still, a number of general observations can be made.

Sources of Innovation

From the early 1970s onward, the deposit-taking industry has experienced the most dramatic period of innovation and change in its history. Moreover, to the outside observer it would appear to be one of the sectors of the economy where new technologies have been changing traditional ways of doing business most rapidly. Deposit-taking institutions have changed the delivery of services to their customers through such devices as the automated teller and pre-authorized payments and also the nature of their services through the daily interest accounts and increasingly sophisticated payments cards.

Despite these dramatic changes in technology, the deposit-taking sector has not been identified as one of the leading sectors for research and development. Indeed, a survey by Statistics Canada in 1984 failed to find any deposit-taking firms that by their definition were performing research and development. The minor importance of research and development in the sector can be attributed in large measure to a question of statistical definition.

Statistics Canada uses a very narrow definition of research and development:

> research and development (R&D) is systematic investigation carried out in the natural and engineering sciences by means of experiment or analysis to achieve a scientific or commercial advance.
>
> Research is original investigation undertaken on a scientific basis to gain new knowledge.
>
> Development is the application of research findings or other scientific knowledge for the creation of new or significantly improved products or processes. If successful, development will usually result in devices or processes which represent an improvement in the "state of the art" and are likely to be patentable (p. 64).

Statistics Canada goes on to state that their definition of research and development follows that of the income tax code, which specifically excludes

> i) market research, sales promotion, ii) quality control or routine analysis and testing of materials, devices and products, iii) research in the social sciences or the humanities,...(v) the commercial production of a new or improved material, device or product or the commercial use of a new or improved process (pp. 64-65).

While in general the terms research and development could refer to activities that take place in the deposit-taking sector, the specific references to "natural and engineering sciences" and to being "patentable" together with the provisions of the tax law exclude many of these development activities in the sector. The deposit-taking sector has dramatically changed the nature of its product and, to an even greater degree, its means of delivery in recent years. This achievement has occurred despite a low level of research and development expenditures in the industry because of the adoption of new technologies that have been developed elsewhere, most notably in the communications and computer industries.

The sources of innovation in the Canadian deposit-taking sector have differed substantially from those in its American counterpart. Only two major innovations in Canada, securitization and the offering of security trading by deposit-taking institutions, have resulted from regulation, while the list is much longer in the U.S. This difference reflects the differences between the countries in terms of the number and degree of the constraints that are embodied in regulations governing deposit-taking institutions. Such features as interest ceilings and restrictions on branching and on interstate banking that have been so prominent in the United States have largely been absent in Canada.

Types of Innovation

Innovation has changed both the processes and the products of the deposit-taking sector, though in two distinct phases. The earliest adoptions of new technology almost exclusively altered processes. Only recently has innovation changed the product of banking. To an extent, this sequence may be explainable; process innovations can be carried out internally without affecting the ways of doing business with customers. The delay in the much heralded revolution in consumer banking has been attributed to customer resistance. The recent overcoming of this resistance remains unexplained.

The two types of innovations have had reinforcing effects on the organization of banks and the resulting patterns of employment. The process innovations that centralized the record keeping function both facilitated and were reinforced by the product innovations. The types of transactions conducted and the types of personnel employed at branches were both changed.

The two types of transactions differ in terms of their impact on measured technology. Process innovation, by definition, is motivated by the desire to reduce costs. To the extent it achieves this goal, process innovation should improve conventional measures of productivity. The effects of product innovation are more difficult to gauge. Many of the innovations that have been discussed can be expected to reduce the time and effort required by customers to obtain the services of financial institutions. The productivity effects of product innovations cannot be captured by conventional measures of productivity because these measures fail to include the costs incurred by customers.

Effects on Industry Organization

Many of the innovations that have been studied can be expected to have substantial implications for the organization of the deposit-taking sector in a number of different ways. Some innovations have clearly changed the internal organization of deposit-taking institutions. Others have changed the activities that are carried out by deposit-taking institutions.

Under the old technology, local branches served to collect and repay deposits and maintain the records of their balances and evaluate and grant loans. Now, many of these functions have been centralized and moved away from the branches. Records of deposits are maintained at computer centres; many entries to deposits are made electronically; transfers and withdrawals can be carried out at locations remote from the branch; and loans are often drawn against pre-authorized lines of credit or negotiated by specialized credit officers at regional centres. These developments have also changed the labour requirements for deposit-taking at the branch and overall. Most clerical functions have been removed from the branch so that the remaining employees are there for the purpose of serving customers. Similarly, the general loan officer has been replaced by specialists who have credit responsibilities for the customers of groups of branches. The need for clerical workers for deposit-taking institutions as a whole has also diminished because tasks that were done manually are now done electronically by computers.

The nature of the deposit-taking industry has also been changed by recent innovations, especially those that have overcome regulatory constraints. The entry of banks into security trading that began with the limited powers gained through the Green Line case will greatly modify the services provided to customers. The trend toward securitization also involves deposit-taking institutions in the supply of new services. Some of the consequences will be internal. Parallel to the new services will be a need for new types of employees, most of whom will be employed at regional centres rather than at branches. Equally important will be the effects on the definition of the industry. Deposit-taking institutions will be performing activities that were once the exclusive preserves of other sectors of the financial industry.

INNOVATION IN THE FUTURE

The dangers of prediction have been amply illustrated by the history of recent technical change in the deposit-taking sector. It illustrates both over-optimism and over-pessimism in predicting the application of innovation. During the mid-1970s, this sector appeared poised for a take-off into a revolution that would fundamentally change the relationship between banks and their customers. Imminent and most notable were automated tellers, point of sale retail terminals, electronic funds transfer, and home banking. All these techniques were in place and operating somewhere, usually in pilot projects, at the time.

This much touted revolution failed to materialize in the way and at the time that many observers predicted. Much innovation was taking place in deposit-taking, but most of it was in-house, affecting processes and not the way products were delivered to customers. Many observers attributed the delay in introducing these innovations to customer resistance rather than any lack of technical knowledge. The pattern reversed itself in the mid-'80s. As seen earlier in this chapter, the installation of ABMs by banks in the two years from April 1983 to April 1985 alone doubled the total number in service. Will similar developments be forthcoming for the other new techniques and services that can be identified? Or is the recent spurt of innovation a one time phenomenon unlikely to be repeated in the near future?

The Ontario Task Force on Employment and New Technology conducted a survey of a sample of chartered banks and trust companies operating in that province with respect to their plans to adopt new technologies. The results are presented for the chartered banks in table 36 and for the trust companies in table 37. These surveys were answered by senior executives and should reflect industry planning and thinking quite well. Each type of institution will be discussed separately as notable differences exist. Moreover, additional attention will be devoted to the replies of the large banks because of their size

Table 36

Adoption of New Technologies by Chartered Banks

	Before 1985		1985–1990		1990–1995	
	Large	All	Large	All	Large	All
Customer Sales and Service Applications						
Automated teller machines	100	43	0	9	33	0
Automatic cheque verification	67	23	33	11	33	21
Pay by phone	0	0	0	9	0	21
Automatic debit/credit systems	100	43	100	21	0	0
Computerized qualification and loan approval	0	25	33	34	0	0
"Smart" cards (with installed microprocessors)	0	0	33	11	33	0
Home banking	0	9	67	21	0	11
Connect to retail point of sale network	33	11	0	32	0	0
Computerized trust management	33	11	0	0	0	0
Computerized pension management	67	23	67	9	0	0
Securities transfer/stockholder services	33	11	0	39	0	0
Design Technologies						
4th generation computer language	33	27	67	39	0	25
Electronic Funds Transfer (EFT)						
EFT interbranch	100	72	0	10	0	0
EFT interbank	100	62	0	0	0	10
EFT corporate	100	44	0	18	0	10
EFT commercial and retail accounts	100	26	0	10	0	0
Office or Office Automation Technologies						
Mainframe/minicomputers	100	75	0	16	0	0
Word processing	100	100	0	16	0	0
Electronic filing	33	11	100	91	0	0
Microcomputers/personal computers	67	89	33	27	0	0
Internal database management systems	100	59	0	48	0	0
Local area networks	0	0	100	91	0	0
Computerized decision support networks	33	27	100	59	0	0
Voice activated computers	0	0	33	27	33	11
Artificial intelligence/expert systems	0	0	33	11	33	11
Integrated work stations	33	11	67	64	0	16
Telecommunications Technologies						
Private automatic branch exchange	100	66	0	0	0	25
Electronic mail	67	39	33	52	33	27
Voice mail	33	11	67	39	0	9
Facsimile with built-in microprocessor	67	39	33	43	0	16
Satellite/microwave systems	33	11	0	0	0	0
Videotex	67	23	0	0	33	11
Video conferencing	0	0	100	59	0	25
Fibre optics	0	0	33	27	0	0

Source: *Ontario Task Force on Employment and Technology*, p. 28.

Note: "0" used prior to 1985 to indicate "have not adopted" and after 1985 to indicate respondents, at the time of the survey, are not planning to adopt this technology or "don't know."

Table 37

Adoption of New Technologies by Trust Companies

	Before 1985	1985–1990	1990–1995
Customer Sales and Service Applications			
Automated teller machines	48	61	39
Automatic cheque verification	13	59	0
Pay by phone	0	0	75
Automatic debit/credit systems	36	11	50
Computerized qualification and loan approval	11	89	0
"Smart" cards (with installed microprocessors)	0	0	64
Home banking	0	11	64
Connect to retail point of sale network	0	11	39
Computerized trust management	48	39	11
Computerized pension management	48	39	11
Securities transfer/stockholder services	48	11	39
Design Technologies			
4th generation computer language	23	61	39
Electronic Funds Transfer (EFT)			
EFT interbranch	23	61	39
EFT interbank	23	36	39
EFT corporate	0	36	39
EFT commercial and retail accounts	0	36	39
Office or Office Automation Technologies			
Mainframe/minicomputers	100	11	11
Word processing	100	11	11
Electronic filing	0	100	11
Microcomputers/personal computers	100	11	11
Internal database management systems	75	64	11
Local area networks	39	61	11
Computerized decision support networks	36	36	39
Voice activated computers	0	0	89
Artificial intelligence/expert systems	0	11	52
Integrated work stations	0	73	39
Telecommunications Technologies			
Private automatic branch exchange	36	75	11
Electronic mail	0	75	11
Voice mail	0	23	64
Facsimile with built-in microprocessor	0	39	48
Satellite/microwave systems	0	25	39
Videotex	0	48	39
Video conferencing	0	75	11
Fibre optics	0	36	0

Source: *Ontario Task Force on Employment and Technology*, p. 70.

Note: "0" used prior to 1985 to indicate "have not adopted" and after 1985 to indicate respondents, at the time of the survey, are not planning to adopt this technology or "don't know." Responses are not mutually exclusive.

and because the smaller banks consist of Schedule B banks that are limited in their activities.

Innovations Planned by the Banks

The responses of the banks indicate the scope of the change in banking in recent years. All large banks offer automated teller service, automatic debit/credit systems, and electronic funds transfer to all classes of customers. They have also integrated computer technology in their internal management. A majority of the larger banks use electronic mail, FAX, and videotext. Up to 1985, only one large bank had connected with point of sale retail terminals.

A number of areas of innovation are indicated for the period 1985-90. The remaining large banks plan to introduce point of sale terminals, and all the large banks plan to add computerized loan qualification and approval. They also plan to adopt new office automation technologies in the form of electronic filing, local area networks, and computerized decision support networks, and new telecommunication technology in the form of voice mail and video conferencing.

Banks, as a whole, do not appear to have major plans for innovation during the period 1990-95. By that time, the major foreseeable innovations in customer service—automatic tellers, point of sale terminals and electronic funds transfer—will be in place. The remaining product innovations to be implemented consist of pay by phone, smart cards and home banking. Of these, only home banking appears likely to be adopted by as much as a majority of the large banks. It is not clear whether this apparent slowing of the pace of innovation in the future indicates a lack of new possibilities or a limited planning horizon for the banks.

Innovations Planned by Trust Companies

The pattern of innovation differed slightly for the trust companies relative to the banks. Some differences, such as the uniform adoption of computerized trust management, pension management and securities transfer, reflect the role of trust companies in trust activities. Like the banks, large trust companies had installed ABMs and automatic cheque verification and had utilized computers in internal administration. The main difference, the limited use of telecommunications, may be the result of the smaller size of the branch networks of trust companies.

The rate of innovation planned by trust companies for the 1985-90 and the 1990-95 periods exceeds that planned by the chartered banks. Some of this innovation will be a catching up. Trust companies are split between the periods 1985-90 and 1990-95 for offering electronic funds transfer and using telecommunications technology. On the other hand, the trust companies appear as if they will be leaders in the introduction of home banking, pay by phone and smart cards.

Innovation: A Cloudy Ball

A review of the plans of deposit-taking institutions with respect to innovation suggest that they are emerging from a period of remarkable innovation into a period of consolidation. Major innovations derived from computer and communications technology have altered the delivery of banking services. While several possible innovations—home banking and pay by phone— offer the same potential to further alter the consumer side of the industry, the majority of firms in the industry do not appear to have plans to implement them. The innovations in the industry will probably take a different form. Deposit-taking institutions will likely use the computer to offer financial instruments that meet their customers' needs with respect to interest terms, maturity, and other characteristics.

NOTE

1. The distinction is frequently made between "online" and "offline" banking machines. An online machine is connected with a computer elsewhere so it can exchange information while processing the customer's transaction. An offline machine is limited to the information that it has available or that is present in the customer's bank card.

Chapter 8

POLICY AND THE
DEPOSIT-TAKING SECTOR

This study has assessed deposit-taking institutions from the perspective of a so-called industry study using a framework that could be applied to any sector of the economy. It has examined deposit-taking institutions as producers of services and as employers of labour. It has reviewed the industry's structure, the types of enterprises in the industry, their ownership and their affiliations with other sectors in the economy; and it has surveyed the forces of innovation and change that have been so prominent in the industry. The output of the deposit-taking sector consists of services to their customers rather than physical goods. Many observers are worried about the increasing importance of service industries in the economy and feel that government action may be required to overcome undesirable consequences of this trend.

The present study has been designed to address many of the concerns of those who are worried about the growth of the service industries. The next section of this chapter considers a number of major policy issues that have been raised with respect to the growth of service industries such as the quality of employment, the regional distribution of activity, and the changing nature of the industry and its product.

The deposit-taking industry, as discussed in chapter 2, is one of the most heavily regulated industries in the Canadian economy. Government involvement so pervades the deposit-taking sector that it is impossible to review the sector as a service industry without at the same time examining the regulations that govern the industry. At present, this need is more urgent for several reasons. First, it is becoming increasingly apparent that the current system of deposit insurance is inappropriate to its objectives. Secondly, the system of regulations is undergoing changes that can fundamentally alter the deposit-taking sector and other sectors closely related to it. The purpose of this discussion is not to indicate yet another blueprint for the reform of the financial system; rather it is to show that policy with respect to the deposit-taking sector as a service industry cannot be formulated without an awareness of the issues involved in prudential regulation.

SERVICE SECTOR POLICY: THE DEPOSIT-TAKING SECTOR

The growth of the service sector has been one of the most noticeable features of the Canadian and other developed economies in recent years. Does this change in output away from traditional production of goods toward the production of services bring with it a need for greater or different types of government involvement in the economy? At a simple level the answer seems clear: both goods and services are produced to satisfy the demands of purchasers. Whether the product has a physical existence as a good should matter little if customers are eager to demand services. Still, policy concerns may be justified at a more subtle level. Possibly the concern arises with respect to the growth of the service sector because service industries share common characteristics that require different policies than are necessary for industries that produce goods. The remainder of this section examines the performance with respect to a number of indicators that have been raised in the service sector debate.

Quality of Employment[1]

This study has examined a number of dimensions of employment in the deposit-taking sector over the period 1960 to 1985. All measures used in the study show that the deposit-taking sector has become an increasingly important employer in the economy during this period. At the beginning of this period of expansion, the deposit-taking sector paid much lower wages than the industrial sector as a whole and concentrated its hiring among high school leavers or drop-outs, offering few chances for advancement beyond the lowest clerical levels. The expansion of employment in the sector has accompanied an improvement in all of these dimensions of quality of employment.

Earnings in the financial industry, the closest measure available over the period, were only 86 percent of the industrial composite earnings in 1960 but were above those in other service industries by 24 percent. By 1985, earnings in the financial industry had grown to exceed the industrial composite and further increased its margin over earnings in other service industries.

The 1971 census shows that the deposit-taking sector concentrated its employment among persons with grades 11, 12 and 13 education by a margin of 82 percent to 50 percent relative to all industry. At the same time, the sector employed relatively fewer persons than all industry at the two extremes of educational attainment—less than grade 9 and university degree.

By 1980, employment in the deposit-taking sector had shifted toward more highly educated personnel. The proportion of employees with only high school education decreased by 26 percentage points to 56 percent compared with the 8 percentage point decrease to 50 percent for industry as a whole. The entire decrease has been reflected in the proportion of employees with some university or with a degree, which has increased from 14 percent to 42 percent of employment in the deposit-taking sector.

Finally, as shown by the structure of employment by organization level for the banks, the opportunities for advancement appear to have improved in the deposit-taking sector in recent years. The proportion of employees in the lowest category, administrative support, has declined from 55.8 to 51.6 percent. In addition, the next lowest category, junior management/supervisory, has also declined from 33.4 to 31.9 percent. All of this decline in the proportion of lower level positions has resulted in an increase in the second highest level, middle management, from 9.3 to 15.1 percent.

All of the above measures suggest that the quality of employment in the deposit-taking sector improved during the period under study. It is not clear what, if any, labour market policies would have been desirable if employment in the deposit-taking sector had been found to offer low quality jobs or if the quality of employment had deteriorated. Fortunately, such speculation is unnecessary because the deposit-taking sector has offered its employees improved quality of employment that compares favourably in earnings to industry at large.

Regional Dimensions

As discussed in chapter 4, the pattern of employment in the deposit-taking sector has been determined in the past by the need to staff local branches in order to provide services for customers. The adoption of new computer technologies has increased the flexibility of deposit-taking institutions in the location of their personnel.

Substantial changes in the regional distribution of employment appear to have accompanied the removal of the constraints imposed by the previous technology. The evidence presented in chapter 4 shows that over the period 1978 to 1984 employment in the deposit-taking sector has increased in Ontario and the Western provinces while decreasing in the Maritimes and Quebec. These shifts have tended to further concentrate the employment of the deposit-taking sector, at least provincially.

Do these changing patterns of employment in the deposit-taking sector require government action? In answer to this question, it is important to recognize the source of these changes. The employment opportunities in the industry have, in effect, become liberated from the constraints of the past. Now, employment will be increasingly influenced by factors such as costs and the availability of qualified labour. The influence of both these factors would appear to be desirable. The increased ability of deposit-taking institutions to lower costs by choice of location of employment should eventually be beneficial to their customers. Similarly, the increased responsiveness of location to the availability of qualified labour gives potential employees greater choice in places to live. Both these factors appear to call for the absence of government measures to influence the location of employment in the deposit-taking sector.

Innovation

Innovation has substantially changed the product of the deposit-taking industry and the way in which it is delivered to customers. Changes, such as seen in this industry, inevitably create anxieties. Will innovation produce a less satisfactory product for the bulk, or even a substantial, portion of customers? Will innovation change the technology of the industry in ways that will harm the degree of competition?

The effects of innovation on the services of the deposit-taking sector were reviewed in chapter 7. Many of the innovations, such as bank cards and ATMs, have increased the convenience of the services available to most customers. Similarly, new instruments, such as daily interest accounts, open mortgages and securitized borrowing, have allowed customers to choose investment or borrowing instruments that more closely suit their needs. On the whole, new products and processes have supplemented and not displaced the traditional products of the deposit-taking sector.[2]

The effects of innovation on the structure of the deposit-taking industry were widely feared as likely to reduce the degree of competition in an industry that was generally characterized as uncompetitive. The need for computer technology, it was thought, would require indivisible capital investments of such a scale that smaller institutions would be unable to compete. The introduction of computer technology, as it occurred, did not fulfill these expectations. Instead, many of the innovations, including those using computer applications, have come first from smaller institutions such as trust companies and credit unions. In addition, the interchanges among ATMs, in contrast to the former cheque clearing arrangements, include many smaller institutions on the same basis as any others.

Neither of the concerns with respect to problems arising from innovation in the deposit-taking sector appear to have been realized as a result of recent developments in the industry. The absence of problems on the consumer side is not unexpected. Unless new developments reflect customers' perceived needs, they are unlikely to be profitable. The absence of competitive problems may be more surprising. Computer technology, contrary to expectations, appears to have enhanced the competitive ability of many smaller institutions. Innovation and changing technology in the deposit-taking sector has not created any need for new or more extensive regulation of this service industry.

PRUDENTIAL REGULATION

Government regulation plays a larger role in determining the character of the deposit-taking industry than almost any other industry. All deposit-taking institutions come under regulations that govern the type of business they can undertake and the requirements for conducting this business. In addition, most deposit-taking institutions are required to gain protection under deposit insurance or comparable systems of guarantees.

Deposit Insurance

The government guarantee of bank deposits through deposit insurance is usually justified on one of several related grounds. Historically, deposit insurance was introduced in the United States to provide stability to the banking system through the prevention of runs that might occur when the failure of one bank creates doubts about the soundness of others. Deposit insurance prevents such runs by giving assurance to depositors about the security of its deposits. Deposit insurance is also justified because of the central role of bank deposits as part of the economy's medium of payment. Any impairment of the payments system supposedly will impose unacceptably large costs on the rest of the economy. Finally, it is argued that deposit insurance protects small depositors against losses. The special concern for small depositors arises because, relative to the size of their deposits, it is very costly for them to assess the risks of different financial institutions.

It appears clear, especially in light of the experience in the United States, that deposit insurance has succeeded in maintaining the stability of the banking system. Bank runs have become a phenomenon of the past. The avoidance of system instability has been accompanied by several forces that increase the risk of failure of insured institutions. Deposit insurance reduces the vigilance of depositors with respect to risk. It also reduces the incentives for the management of financial institutions to avoid risk.

In the absence of deposit insurance, customers of financial institutions must attempt to assess the risk of failure of any institution at which they hold their funds. If institutions are perceived to have different levels of risk, depositors will require higher deposit rates from riskier institutions in order to compensate for the greater probability of loss. The presence of deposit insurance alters the customer's incentives substantially. Up to the maximum limit for insured deposits, all deposit institutions can be regarded as identical by customers. Even above the limits for deposit insurance, the differences among institutions are reduced. The presence of insurance for a substantial proportion of deposits at any institution protects its uninsured depositors against instability of the institution arising from massive withdrawals of deposits. In addition, deposit insurers have paid off uninsured deposits in many instances when a financial institution has failed.

Deposit insurance also affects the incentives facing the managements of financial institutions. In its absence, the choice among investment policies will be made with an awareness that customers will require a higher rate of return on deposits to the extent that they perceive greater risks from the firm's policies. The management then must compare the possible higher returns from the riskier policy with the higher costs of funds. The presence of deposit insurance blunts this incentive. Most depositors are protected regardless of the institution's investment policy. When a large proportion of deposits are fully insured, the choice of a riskier investment policy will have little impact on an institution's cost of funds. Management may now be more inclined to pursue the riskier policy because it would have a smaller effect on its cost of funds.

The effects of these forces can be seen most clearly by comparing the competitive position of an institution pursuing a safe investment policy before and after the introduction of deposit insurance. Before deposit insurance, this institution was able to maintain lower interest rates than other institutions because of its greater safety. After the introduction, it will have to pay the same rates as the institutions that pursue riskier investment policies.

Deposit insurance presents a paradox in terms of its different effects at the system and institutional levels. While it reduces both system risk and the threat to any institution from system risk, it also reduces the sensitivity of depositors toward risk and tempers the disincentives to management in taking risk. This paradox creates problems for the design of any system of deposit insurance. The degree of risk undertaken by financial institutions in the absence of insurance may not be a good indicator of the risks chosen with insurance.

The degree to which deposit insurance alters the incentives of depositors and the management of financial institutions to take greater risk depends on the design of the insurance. The Canadian system has a number of features that tend to exacerbate the problem. The fixed premium for deposit insurance means that insured institutions do not bear the same costs for undertaking risks as they did before deposit insurance. At present, the only cost is the increased probability of failure and the resulting losses to shareholders. In the absence of deposit insurance, the institution would also face a higher cost of funds as its riskiness increased. In addition, the deposit insurers have also generally protected all depositors, insured and uninsured, and in some cases shareholders, after the failure of an institution with insured deposits. This extension of insurance beyond its legal limits has the same effect on uninsured creditors as insurance has on depositors. They have less need to assess the riskiness of the financial institution where they place their money.

Recent Experience

Many of these concerns about the effects of deposit insurance could have been dismissed as academic as recently as the early 1980s. While deposit insurance had been introduced in 1967 in response to the failure of several financial institutions in Ontario, the subsequent experience suggested that the programme was working well. Several failures of small institutions had occurred, but these had been handled by CDIC without any problems. The experience from 1983 onward has been completely different, with failure of 12 trust and loan companies and two chartered banks—the first bank failures in Canada since 1923. In addition, as mentioned earlier, mergers were arranged for three clearly troubled banks. In one case, the absorption of Bank of B.C. by Hong Kong and Shanghai Bank, the $200 million of financial assistance from CDIC formed part of the terms of the merger.

Table 37 documents the failures of insured deposit-taking institutions from 1980 to 1985 and indicates the factors that contributed to these failures. This table shows that management failures of a variety of types have contributed to every one of the failures listed. The authors of *A Framework for Financial Regulation*, a report to the Economic Council of Canada concluded: "imprudent management, in the final analysis, is almost always the dominant cause of financial failure" (p. 46). As discussed, deposit insurance, by its very presence, reduces the incentives for prudent management.

Proposals for Reform of Deposit Insurance

Dissatisfaction with the recent problems of deposit insurance in Canada has produced a number of proposals for reform. Reform could be directed toward any of three areas: sharing of risks by insured depositors, setting premiums, or the treatment of uninsured depositors on the failure of an institution.

Table 38
Factors that Contributed to the Failure of Various Financial Institutions, Canada, 1980 to 1985

	Year	Internal Factors Management Errors					Questionable practices	External Factors economic environment
		Inadequate management of assets	Inadequate management of liabilities	Insufficient diversification	Mismanagement of assets and liabilities	Erosion of the capital base		
Chartered Banks								
Canadian Commercial Bank	1985	x	x			x	x	x
Northland Bank	1985	x	x			x	x	x
Federally Chartered Trust and Loan Companies								
Astra Trust	1980	x		x			x	
Dial Mortgage Loan	1981	x						
Fidelity Trust	1983			x			x	x
Greymac Mortgage	1983	x					x	x
Seaway Mortgage	1983	x					x	x
Northguard Mortgage	1983	x						
Pioneer Trust	1985	x				x	x	x
Western Capital Trust	1985	x				x	x	x
Continental Trust	1985	x			x		x	x
Provincially Chartered Trust and Mortgage Companies								
Greymac Mortgage	1983	x					x	
Seaway Trust	1983	x					x	
Crown Trust	1983	x					x	
London Loan	1983	x						

Source: *A Framework for Financial Regulation*, Economic Council, 1987, p. 47.

Sharing risks

The majority of the proposals have concentrated on risk sharing by depositors through co-insurance. The green paper from the Department of Finance and the Wyman committee report both propose insurance covering only 90 percent of deposits up to a limit of $100,000 per account. The Senate committee and the Dupre task force both recommend staggered co-insurance with the degree of protection decreasing with the size of the deposit.

The co-insurance approach to reform is subject to a limitation inherent in each of these proposals. Any significant sharing of risk with depositors offsets the benefits that accrue from deposit insurance, reducing system stability, rendering the payments system more vulnerable and reducing the protection for small depositors. Yet, paradoxically, a significant sharing of risk would be required to create effective incentives for depositors and institutions to avoid risks. These problems were apparently recognized in that none of the proposals suggest any major shifting of risk toward insured depositors.

Risk-related premiums

A system of risk-related premiums for deposit insurance was proposed by the Economic Council of Canada in 1976. Adoption of this plan would mean that the premiums paid for deposit insurance by any institution would depend on its risk as perceived by the deposit insurer. Ideally, the variable premiums would simulate the additional returns that would have to be paid to induce depositors to accept risk in the absence of deposit insurance. Variable rate premiums for deposit insurance have been criticized in Canada and elsewhere for being attractive in principle but impossible to implement in practice. The regulators supposedly would lack the information about risks of different investments required to set the premiums.

This criticism of variable rate deposit insurance reflects a failure to understand both the features of the present system of regulation and the way in which variable rate deposit insurance could be implemented. The present fixed rate premium can be considered as an extreme case of a variable rate in which all risks are considered equal. In contrast, the accompanying regulation governing the activities of financial institutions is based on precisely the opposite assumption: some activities are too risky for financial institutions to undertake at all, others are subject to strict limits, and still others may be carried out freely. Requests or requirements that financial institutions maintain specific capital ratios reflect regulators' judgements of risk. Thus, the current approach to controlling the risks of financial institutions depends on the regulators' knowledge of risk in the same way as variable rate deposit insurance would. The difference is that the need for information, though equally present, is less explicit.

The information needs of variable rate deposit insurance arise from the need to set deposit insurance premiums in advance. The information needs would be reduced if deposit insurance premiums could be set after the contributions of various actions to the overall risk were known. A modification of a variable rate system has been proposed by which premiums could be adjusted after the fact once the riskiness of assets has been revealed. Such a procedure could be objected to on two grounds: it causes undue uncertainty for financial institutions, and the adjustment of the premium would not be possible for financial institutions that fail. Both of these criticisms can be answered.

The uncertainty for deposit institutions requires them to assess the risks themselves carefully in order for them to predict the consequences of their actions. In many cases, the financial institutions will be as well or better placed than the regulators to appraise risks, especially for new activities. Thus, requiring the institutions to assess the risks themselves overcomes part of the information requirements for the regulators.

The objection that payments after the fact will not have any impact on failing institutions has only limited force. The failure of institutions is a relatively infrequent event. As a result, institutions will attach a probability to the payment of premiums after the fact for undertaking risky activities weighted by their probability of survival. Given the rarity of failure, the prospect of paying the adjusted premium after the fact should serve to give an incentive to assess their risks accurately.

Variable rate deposit insurance need not be viewed as a complete replacement for the present system of regulation. The differences in premiums may never capture the differences in risk among different activities precisely. Yet, even with some simple differences in premiums, the riskiness of assets can be recognized and reflected in the costs of financial institutions. Still, the system of deposit insurance could be bolstered by a system of regulation in many ways similar to that existing at present.

The combination of variable rate deposit insurance with regulation offers a flexibility that is essentially absent in the present system of regulation. Substantial discontinuities in existing regulations permit certain activities up to specified limits. In effect, the dollar of such an activity beyond the last permitted dollar is treated as if it were an unacceptable risk, whereas the last permitted dollar was riskless. This treatment is misleading in that the last permitted dollar differs little in risk from the next dollar. The use of variable rate deposit insurance permits a more gradual approach in reflecting the risk. For example, the first 1 percent of a portfolio held in a risky asset may not cause any increase in deposit insurance charges per dollar of deposits, the second percent may raise the charge slightly, and further holdings would cause still higher insurance charges at the margin. Not only does this pricing structure offer greater flexibility, it also likely reflects the impact of successive holdings on the overall risk of financial institutions.

Limits to coverage

Deposit insurance, in practice, affects more than just insured depositors. The incentives of other groups are affected by their expectations of the measures to be taken when failure of an insured institution becomes imminent. The authorities are committed to meet the claims of insured depositors but can act in a variety of ways with respect to uninsured depositors, other creditors and shareholders. Honouring only insured deposits would be the most drastic measure that could be taken by the insurers. At the other extreme, an arranged takeover by a healthy bank with some compensation of the shareholders of the failing bank would be the most lenient. This alternative would protect the interests of uninsured depositors and other creditors.

With deposit insurance, incentives still exist for uninsured creditors to assess risks in holding their funds at any institution and to determine whether they are justified by the additional return. Indeed, some proposals for the reform of deposit insurance suggest that insured institutions be required to issue a certain amount of uninsured debt to control the risks accepted by management. To the extent that deposit insurance provides implicit protection to these groups, they will have diminished incentives in the same ways as insured depositors, increasing the risks to the deposit insurer.

The CDIC has not pursued a consistent policy with respect to treatment of failing institutions. At one extreme, CDIC has in the case of small regional trust companies restricted its coverage to insured deposits, with holders of uninsured deposits and shareholders suffering losses. In other cases, CDIC protected all deposits without regard to their coverage under the legal limits to deposit insurance.[3] Finally, in the case of the Bank of B.C., CDIC contributed to assist the merger even though assets were left available for distribution to shareholders. This practice of extending coverage beyond insurance limits on a selective basis can be questioned on grounds of fairness and fiscal responsibility. But far more important, it blunts the incentive mechanisms that protect financial institutions against failure.

Enforcement of the limits to deposit insurance appears to be a difficult step in practice. Deposit insurers and other regulators must act when, though the probabilities are strong, it is not absolutely certain that an institution is insolvent. Rights of shareholders and uninsured creditors will be jeopardized by premature liquidation of an insured institution. On the other hand, extension of protection beyond the defined limits is antithetical to the functioning of a sound system of deposit insurance. Reform of deposit insurance must include two elements: clear criteria for the initiation of action by the deposit insurer and other regulators when failure of an institution becomes imminent;[4] and a prohibition on payments to uninsured depositors, other creditors and shareholders until the CDIC has recovered all expenses that it has incurred in compensating insured depositors.

THE REFORM OF REGULATION

The regulation of deposit-taking institutions has been built around a number of key elements. The central element of the system of prudential regulation has been the policy of restrictive entry. In particular, the activity of banking has been limited, for the most part, to firms that are distinctly separate from other financial institutions and from firms that carry out real economic activity. Since 1967, this separation has been achieved by limiting the ownership by any single interest to 10 percent of a Schedule A chartered bank. The separation has been reinforced further by keeping banks out of the central activities of other financial institutions. In the case of trust companies, though entry requirements have been less severe, their powers as deposit-taking institutions have been more limited than banks.

This approach taken in Canada to the regulation of chartered banks can be described as a market restricting approach in that it "governs the conditions under which enterprises become eligible to be certified as a particular type of financial institution or to carry on some type of financial activity" (Chant, p. 322). In effect, it defines the market and its participants. Prudential regulation, an alternative to market regulation, "refers to the set of rules that govern the activities of enterprises participating within the industry and can be considered as similar to safety regulations of the airline industry" (Chant, p. 322). Greater emphasis has been placed on prudential regulation in the rules governing trust and loan companies and credit unions relative to banks.

Market restricting regulation and prudential regulation differ with respect to their effects on the regulated market. Market restricting regulation reduces competition by limiting the participants to any market, but it leaves their powers relatively unrestricted. Prudential regulation permits a larger number of entrants but governs their activity more closely.

The emphasis on market regulation in Canada has been severely questioned, first, by the Porter Commission in 1964 and, subsequently, by the Economic Council in 1976. The Royal Commission on Banking and Finance argued "that the Bank Act be extended to cover a wide group of institutions which are now engaged in the business of banking, that those not coming under the legislation be prohibited from undertaking this business and that a broader range of lending powers be granted to all lending institutions...our recommendations would permit the savings banks and trust, loan and other companies coming under the banking legislation to compete for commercial and personal lending business" (1964:563).

In a similar vein, the Economic Council argued "that the federal and provincial governments adopt an approach to the regulation of deposit institutions whereby the rules governing an institution should relate to the activities or functions undertaken by that institution" (1976:132). The Economic Council's recommendation would apply prudential regulation to an institution according to the functions it undertakes.

In 1986, the federal government revealed proposals for reform of financial legislation in its New Directions for the Financial Sector. The main thrust of the proposals was the extension of ownership limitations to trust and mortgage loan companies, though some easing of ownership restrictions for small banks was proposed. In particular, the rules suggested for trust and loan companies include the following provisions:

> Approval for the incorporation of new trust [and] loan companies will be restricted to applicants with no significant commercial interests.
>
> Commercial interests will not be permitted to acquire or increase significant ownership positions in non-bank institutions with capital in excess of $450 million.
>
> Such larger non-bank institutions with commercial links will be required to have at least 35 per cent of their voting shares publicly traded and widely held by December 31, 1991, or within five years of reaching the $50 million capital threshold.
>
> Trust [and] loan...companies with no commercial links and with capital in excess of $750 million will also be required to have at least 35 per cent of their voting shares publicly traded and widely held by December 31, 1991, or within five years of reaching the $750 million capital threshold. Once the threshold is exceeded, no shareholder will be able to acquire an ownership position in the institution in excess of 10 per cent and significant shareholders will not be permitted to increase their ownership positions.

The proposals represent a recommitment to the principle of separation of ownership of financial institutions from other economic activity and greater reliance on market regulation.

Policies for the regulation of financial institutions generally involve a mixture of market restricting and prudential regulation. Each achieves its objectives only at some cost. Market restricting policies reduce competition in different activities by restricting entry, whereas prudential regulation constrains the choices that can be made by management of existing firms. Already the emphasis in Canada on market restricting policies exceeds that in most other market economies. Further emphasis on this approach appears questionable at this time, particularly in light of the often expressed concern for the undue concentration in the Canadian banking system.

The particular approach proposed by the government has a further undesirable effect in addition to its effects on entry. The proposals will also stifle competition for the management of major financial institutions. This competition in the form of the corporate take-over serves as a powerful mechanism for the discipline and replacement of managements of inefficient firms. If outside groups feel able to run the firm more efficiently than existing management, they can buy control and gain the benefits of better management through the appreciation of the value of the firm. At present, the managements of Schedule A banks are insulated from this mechanism by the 10 percent ceiling on the shareholdings of any single interest. The government's proposals will now extend this protection to the incumbent management of trust and mortgage loan companies at the cost of potential inefficiencies in years to come.

A blueprint for the regulation of deposit-taking institutions falls far beyond the scope of this study. Nevertheless, a number of desirable elements can be specified. Easier entry and greater competition for management and control should be fostered through easing the proposed restrictions on ownership of deposit-taking institutions. Problems of conflict of interest and self-dealing should be dealt with directly by a combination that involves a strengthening of prudential regulation directed at undesirable or questionable practices, the use of variable deposit insurance premiums, and the imaginative use of other devices such as continuing liability for certain transactions that are not at arm's length. Such an approach would have the potential to enhance competition in financial markets without endangering the safety and stability of the system.

NOTES

1. All the results in this section have been drawn from chapter 4.

2. The development of ATMs may have made some branches uneconomic and led to their closing. Generally, Canadian deposit-taking institutions have been criticized for having too many, not too few, branches.

3. The argument may be made that the assisted merger is the cheapest way for the CDIC to protect the interests of insured depositors in some instances.

4. Such a proposal has been made by the government in its *New Directions for the Financial Sector*. It recommends that CDIC be given the power to take control of a regulated financial institution when insolvency threatens.

BIBLIOGRAPHY

Bank of Canada, *Bank of Canada Review*, various issues.

Bank for International Settlements (1986), *Recent Innovations in International Banking*, Basle: Bank for International Settlements.

Binhammer, H. and J. Williams (1976), *Deposit-Taking Institutions: Innovation and the Process of Change*, Ottawa, Ministry of Supply and Services.

Boadway, R. and H. Kitchen (1984), *Canadian Tax Policy*, 2nd edition, Toronto: Canadian Tax Foundation, Canadian Tax Paper no.76.

Canada (1980), *Banks and Banking Law Revision Act, 1980*.

_____ (1971), *Census of Canada, vol. 3 (part 3) Economic Characteristics: Labour Force*.

_____ (1981), *Census of Canada, Population: Economic Characteristics*.

Canada Deposit Insurance Corporation (1986), *Annual Report*.

Canada Gazette, *Returns of the Chartered Banks to the Minister of Finance*, various issues.

Canadian Bankers' Association, *Financial Statistics*, various issues.

_____ (1986), *Credit Card Operations of the Chartered Banks in Canada*.

_____ (1984), *Trends in Employment, Canada's Chartered Banks*.

Canadian Payments Association (1986), *Directory*, vol. 1.

Canadian Master Tax Guide (1987), Don Mills: CCH Canadian Limited.

Chant, J. (1985), "Economic prerequisites to the Deregulation of Financial Institutions," in J. Ziegel et. al., *Canadian Financial Institutions: Changing the Regulatory Environment*, Toronto: Ontario Economic Council.

_____ (forthcoming), "Financial Institutions and Tax Reform."

Department of Regional Industrial Expansion, Commercial Services Directorate, Service Industries and Consumers Goods Branch (1987), "Employment Dynamics: Focus on Canada's Service Sector."

Department of Finance (1985), *The Regulation of Canadian Financial Institutions: Proposals for Discussion*, Ottawa: Ministry of Supply and Services (referred to as the green paper).

Dunsmore, R. (1985), "Employment Law," *The Financial Times*, November 17, p. 2.

Economic Council of Canada (1987), *A Framework for Financial Regulation*, Ottawa: Ministry of Supply and Services.

_____ (1976), *Efficiency and Regulation*, Ottawa: Ministry of Supply and Services.

Financial Post 500 (1986).

Geehan, R. and L. Allen (1978), "Measuring the real output and productivity of savings and credit institutions," *Canadian Journal of Economics*, vol. XI, no. 4, pp. 670-79.

House of Commons, Finance Committee (1982), "Profit Situation of the Chartered Banks," *Minutes of the Proceedings*, no. 109.

Institute for Research in Public Policy (1986), Symposium on "Conceptual and Data Issues in Trade in Services," *Working Paper*.

Jenkins, G. (1977), *Inflation: Its Financial Impact on Business in Canada*, Ottawa: Ministry of Supply and Services.

Landy, L. (1980), "Financial Innovation in Canada," *Federal Reserve Bank of New York Quarterly Review*, vol. 5, no. 3, pp. 1-8.

Lowe G. (1981), "The Causes of Unionization," *Relations Industrielles*, vol. 36, no. 4, pp. 863-92.

_____ (1980), *Bank Unionization in Canada: A Preliminary Analysis*, Toronto: Centre for Industrial Relations, University of Toronto.

Minister of Finance (1987), *Tax Reform 1987: Income Tax Reform*.

Minister of State for Finance (1986), *New Directions for the Financial Sector*.

Mintz, J. (1978), *The Measure of Profitability in Canadian Banking*, Ottawa: Ministry of Supply and Services.

Ontario Task Force on Employment and Technology (1985), *Employment and New Technology in the Chartered Banks and Trust Industry: An Appendix to the Final Report*, Toronto: Ontario Government.

Ponak, A. and L. Moore (1981), "Chartered Bank Unionism: Perspectives and Issues," *Relations Industrielles*, vol. 36, no. 1, pp. 3-31.

Power A. and D.K. Varma (1984), *The Touche Ross Guide to Financial Reporting for Canadian Banks*, CCH Canadian Limited.

Royal Commission on Banking and Finance (1964), Report, Ottawa: Queen's Printer.

Ruggles, R. and N. Ruggles (1956), *National Income Accounts and Income Analysis*, New York: McGraw-Hill.

_____ (1982), "Integrated Economic Accounts for the United States," *Survey of Current Business*, vol. 62, no. 5, pp. 1-53.

Rymes, T. (1985), "Inflation, non-optimal monetary arrangements and the banking imputation in the national accounts," *Review of Income and Wealth*, 31, pp. 85-96.

_____ (1986), "Further thoughts on the banking imputation in the national accounts," *Review of Income and Wealth*, 32, pp. 425-41.

Silber, W. (1983), "The Process of Financial Intermediation," *American Economic Review*, vol. 73, no. 2, pp. 89-95.

St-Hilaire, F. and J. Whalley (1986), "Some Estimates of Trade Flows in Banking Services," in Institute for Research in Public Policy, Symposium on *Conceptual and Data Issues in Trade and Services: A Selection of Papers*, Ottawa: Institute for Research in Public Policy.

Statistics Canada (71-002), *Employment and Earnings*, various issues.

_____ (61-207), *Corporate Financial Statistics*, various issues.

_____ (61-208), *Corporate Taxation Statistics*, various issues.

_____ (61-006), *Financial Institutions*, various issues.

_____ (61-005), *Gross Domestic Product by Industry*, various issues.

_____ (13-549E), *National Income and Expenditure Accounts*, vol. 3.

_____ (61-516), *Real Domestic Product by Industry*, various issues.

_____ (88-202), *Industrial Research and Development Statistics*.

Stikeman, H. (1985), *Canada Tax Service*, Don Mills: Richard De Boo Publishers.

Sunga, P.S. (1967), "The Treatment of Interest and Net Rents in the National Accounts Framework," *Review of Income and Wealth*, 13, pp. 26-35.

_____ (1984), "An Alternative to the Current Treatment of Interest in the United States and Canadian System of National Accounts," *Review of Income and Wealth*, 30, pp. 385-402.

Toronto Stock Exchange, *Toronto Stock Exchange Review*, various issues.

United States, Department of the Treasury, *Tax Reform for Fairness, Simplicity, and Economic Growth*, vol. 3, Value Added Tax, Washington: Department of the Treasury.

Working Committee on the Canada Deposit Insurance Corporation (1985), *Report*, Ottawa: Supply and Services Canada.